Sunset
French
Cook Book

By the Editors of Sunset Books and Sunset Magazine

Lane Publishing Co. • Menlo Park, California

MATTHEW NAYTHONS

MICHAEL GAULKE

Sunset Went to France...

. . . and the result is the book you hold in your hand. The on-location photos on this page are only a visual sampling of the research and travel that took Sunset's editors to French homes, marketplaces, city restaurants, country inns, and riverbank picnic sites.

Our very warmest *merci* to those whose hospitality and personal effort helped to make this book a reality: Monsieurs and Mesdames Jean Pierre Schmitt, Jean Mourot, L. Morier, Will Kirkman; Philippe de Lattre Rothé; Patrice Lanrezac; Jean Claude Willot; Anne Marie Lyon; Paul Bocuse; Daniel Lecuyer; Marie Claire de la Grandière; Michele Bottard; Francine de Breton; Marie Ange Galliot; Harry Serlis; Jean Lidon, Conseil Inter-profesionel du Vin de Bordeaux; Yves Fourault and Robert Nicholson of Louis Eschenauer S. A.; Mary Lyons, Food and Wines from France, Inc.; George Hern, Jr., Lucetta Sebba, Barbara Hess, French Government Tourist Office.

Book Editors: Jerry Anne Di Vecchio
Home Entertaining Editor, Sunset Magazine

Judith A. Gaulke
Assistant Editor, Sunset Books

Photography: Glenn Christiansen

Artwork: Earl Thollander

Design: JoAnn Masaoka

Executive Editor, Sunset Books: David E. Clark

First printing November 1976. World rights reserved.
Copyright © Lane Publishing Co. • Menlo Park, CA 94025.
Library of Congress No. 76-7666. ISBN Title No. 0-376-02421-6. Lithographed in the United States.

Contents

Getting started 4

The first course 8

Warming soups 15

Fish and shellfish 21

Birds and small game 32

Hearty meats 44

Vegetables and salads 63

Eggs and cheese 72

Breads and desserts 83

Index 95

Metric chart 96

Special features

Apéritifs: a refreshing way to begin 9
Cornichons: little green pickles 13
Homemade broth for a multitude of uses 16
Confit: salt preserved duck 43
Navarin: a party stew 54
French hamburgers 59
Growing sorrel 70
Crème fraîche and fromage blanc: household staples 77
Basic crêpes 81

"There are lots of recipes, but it is the personal feeling added to each that makes a dish individual."

Getting started

Tales of what makes a French chef great often begin with a story about the kitchen of his youth. The recipes he holds most dear may turn out to belong to "grandmother," "aunt," or "father's cousin"—they are the carefully prepared, simple everyday foods of home.

It is this basic French cookery, more closely related to the family than to the intimidatingly complex haute (or high) cuisine, that is the backbone of this book.

Herein are the wisdoms and skills of home cooks who through the years have shared their meals, their kitchens, their markets, and their time to familiarize *Sunset* editors with this practical and delicious view of French food.

Additionally, from restaurants most humble to most highly rated we have gathered dishes that demonstrate delightful simplicities.

You will find dishes you can duplicate with ease, using foods common to our markets; dishes for the family as well as for guests, because the cooking is the down-to-earth, no-nonsense kind. Results, though, are such that even the most discriminating will be appreciative.

Although luxuries like truffles and foie gras (fatted goose liver) do appear extensively in the cuisine of France, you can get along without them very well. A restaurant chef may embellish his grandmother's terrine with truffles, but the essence, unadorned, is still to her credit—and will be to yours, too.

We do offer a few options for including these costly specialties when an occasion warrants, but the basic recipes stand securely at other times.

Don't be surprised if many dishes on these pages have familiar overtones. The French began to influence our tastes even before Benjamin Franklin assumed his diplomatic duties in Paris.

How to serve a meal French-style

"Small portions of good things served in sequence" summarizes the routine of a typical French meal. The main meal of the day may be either lunch or dinner, but both are served in courses. Ordinarily, you begin in one of three ways: with hors d'oeuvres (hot or cold appetizers from the chapter beginning on page 8), with soup (from the chapter beginning on page 15), or with both—hors d'oeuvres, then, are served first. Soup in the evening is more typical than soup at midday.

Then comes the entrée. In times when personal bulk was fashionable, several protein courses were commonplace. Now, such abundance is reserved for special occasions like banquets—and *Larousse Gastronomique* is quite precise about what is proper and in what order, amending that "at the family table full license is permitted."

A vegetable or two accompanies (or is part of) the main dish. You have many main courses from which to choose—the chapter dealing with fish and shellfish begins on page 21, birds and small game on page 32, and hearty meats on page 44. Vegetable dishes begin on page 63.

The French custom is to serve the salad after, not before, the main part of the meal. In this position, "lettuce" and "salad" are synonymous in France, and some tasty examples start on page 71. Salads of other foods are considered hors d'oeuvres and recipes for them are in the chapter that starts on page 8.

In the home, cheese is often served with the salad rather than as a following course. A list of suitable cheeses you can buy is on page 71, and a cheese you can make is on page 76. Crusty bread is automatically on the table throughout the meal, but is savored most with this course.

The meal can end in several ways. The simplest is with a piece of fruit. For more auspicious climaxes, you will find desserts in the chapter dealing with eggs and cheese (page 72) and in the last chapter (page 83)—which also includes directions for making three breads the French buy daily. Lacking a local French baker, you have the option of making these breads yourself.

Generally, coffee and liqueurs are leisurely served away from the dining table.

You can try serving the dishes in courses as the French still do, even though most now manage without servants. Or you can simply serve the meal as you are accustomed to doing.

Do many courses mean many dishes?

Even with their multiple courses, the French family uses no more, and sometimes fewer, dishes than we might with a comparable menu.

The dinner plate acts as a liner for a smaller hors d'oeuvre plate or soup bowl. Or else it holds most of the meal: the appetizer (if it's rather tidy), the bread or roll (more typically placed right on the table), and the salad.

There is usually a fresh plate for dessert. It is not unusual for you to be expected to use the same fork through the meal, except perhaps for dessert.

If both red and white wine are served, you have a glass for each—or make do with just one glass. Bottled mineral water is often on the table. There might be a glass for it, but the wine glass can do double duty.

In French homes, the host likes to present the foods for your viewing—the wit of one cook reflects the importance of the visual with food in the quote on page 83. "Feast the eye before the stomach." (Similar thoughtful comments of cooks we encountered are laced in pencraft throughout the book.)

What about the wine?

When one is drinking great wines of famous chateaux, the matching of food and wine is taken seriously. But for the most part, eating in France confirms the correctness of observing one's own personal taste when choosing the wine. For everyday, almost any wine is preferred to none. In many homes, both red and white are on the table at the same time, if Monsieur prefers one and Madame the other. Openly contradicting formalized rules for wine is very much the French habit.

American jug white and red wines are, as often reported, on a par with, if not considerably better than, France's local vins ordinaires. American varietals finished in ways similar to wines you might encounter in France include the fuller-bodied (often with the flavor of oak) whites such as Pinot Chardonnay, Pinot Blanc, and some dry Sauvignon Blancs. Lighter, but also dry, whites include Folle Blanche, White Pinot, Blanc Fumé (or Fumé Blanc), Sylvaner, Traminer. Reds with a character complementary to French-style foods include Cabernet Sauvignon, Cabernet, Ruby Cabernet, Gamay, Gamay Beaujolais, Pinot Noir, Pinot St. George, Barbera, Carignane, Charbono, Merlot, and Zinfandel.

You can choose from among these wines or research the available wines of France when selecting a beverage for a menu.

One interesting aspect of wine service is its appearance with the salad. Wine experts warn about the disastrous effect a vinegary dressing can have on the palate. Yet in French homes, cheese served with the salad is the perfect buffer.

Isn't French food awfully rich to use routinely?

Those whose primary experience with French food has been at the hands of restaurateurs anywhere in the world, including France, often have the impression that everything floats in butter or is coated with cream.

For day-to-day use, considerable restraint is exercised. This is not to minimize the importance of these ingredients; some dishes are dependent on rich elements—where would hollandaise be without butter, or pots de crème without whipping cream?

But there is a rising tide of calorie awareness even at the haute cuisine level in France. In reality, home cooking has long been cognizant of this consideration. Additionally, even margarine has made inroads.

Lavish foods, though enjoyed, are balanced by eating habits worthy of attention. Fruit is a more routine way to end a meal than is a prepared dessert. Portions are small for entrées; soups and appetizers are often based on vegetables; salad is a daily choice.

Professionally, the "new cuisine" or "slimming cuisine" is limited thus far to only a few adventurous chefs who also look, perhaps, to the kitchens of their youth for inspiration.

Do you need special ingredients to cook French-style?

For the most part, ingredients readily available in a well-stocked supermarket will get you through any recipe in this book.

Dijon mustard is one item mentioned with considerable frequency; it is made in the United States as well as imported from France. Canned (in brine, vinegar, or water) green peppercorns are, perhaps, less familiar; look for them in specialty food stores if they are not in the supermarket. All the herbs and spices specified are packaged by major firms in this country. Shallots are increasingly available, but green or red onions are proposed alternates.

Directions are included for creating or growing other essential, hard-to-come-by items, such as crème fraîche and fromage blanc (page 77), cornichons (page 13), confit de canard (page 43), and sorrel (page 69).

Are special tools necessary?

At right is pictured a collection of kitchen tools that make certain chores easier. Still, you would find in almost any kitchen an alternative piece of equipment for each.

An electric mixer or rotary beater can take the place of a wire whip. Sauce pans, kettles, and frying pans of various materials, styles, and sizes can be used. Fancy molds have plainer alternates. A blender, food mill, or food chopper will do much the same job as a food processor. And so forth.

What these utensils can do is provide the French shape, such as a coeur à la crème mold, brioche mold, or terrine; help to perform a specific chore, such as poach a salmon or bake a cooky over direct heat; or just give the finished dish the French "look" through presentation in gratin dishes and pans, pots de crèmes, quiche molds, or scallop shells.

Special Kitchen Tools

TOOLS that give the French flair or form. From the top: **1)** *hanging rack with detachable hooks;* **2)** *oval metal gratin pan;* **3)** *steel crêpe pan;* **4)** *wooden mallet;* **5)** *oval frying pan or fish sauté pan;* **6)** *copper mixing bowl for egg whites;* **7)** *wire basket for drying lettuce, holding foods;* **8)** *large ceramic mixing bowl;* **9)** *fluted mold for frozen desserts;* **10)** *wire whip;* **11)** *large copper sauté pan or sauteuse;* **12)** *coeur à la crème mold;* **13)** *pots de crème cups;* **14)** *ceramic quiche or tart dish;* **15)** *soufflé dish;* **16)** *oval ceramic terrine;* **17)** *sauce pans;* **18)** *butcher's block;* **19)** *decorative tube molds for baking;* **20)** *French chef knives and paring knives;* **21)** *large aluminum frying pan;* **22)** *escargot pan and clamp;* **23)** *aluminum 2 or 3-egg omelet pan;* **24)** *fish poacher;* **25)** *copper kettles;* **26)** *food processor;* **27)** *madeleine pan;* **28)** *tapered rolling pin;* **29)** *gaufrette iron;* **30)** *roasting pan;* **31)** *round and rectangular terrines;* **32)** *individual and large brioche molds;* **33)** *charlotte mold;* **34)** *ovenproof onion soup bowl;* **35)** *scallop shells;* **36)** *oval baking dish;* **37)** *oval enameled metal and ceramic gratin dishes;* **38)** *decorated oval pâté mold or terrine.*

"With the country foods, drink the country wines."

The first course

Tasty food served to titillate the appetite as well as appease it—that's our definition of hors d'oeuvres, the French word that is equally understood in English as something to be served before a meal.

We might reserve a first course for special occasions only, but for a French family hors d'oeuvres are a daily routine—a custom you'll probably find easy to adopt.

Interestingly, you may find the inclusion of a first course a way to make menu planning simpler. A high protein appetizer (often made well ahead of time) can add substance to a light meal of scrambled eggs, sandwiches, or a quick soup when you are in a hurry. Or appetizers, French-style, can add fresh thinking: vegetables presented as a first course bring variety to an element of the meal that often challenges a cook.

The French certainly set a wide range of standards for appetizers—from the simplicity of a hard-cooked egg or a few olives to the elegance and luxury of foie gras (the whole livers of specially raised geese). Foie gras is incredibly rich, delicate, and smooth, setting the standards by which all liver pâtés may be measured. Available canned or in jars, at eye-opening prices, foie gras is also used to flavor pâtés made of other livers, and cost is indicative of the proportions. But for pleasing the palate as well as the purse, home cooks have everyday solutions, such as the chicken liver pâté reported here, which is exceptional in its own right.

The French also have a great appreciation for well-flavored meat or fish dishes as a prelude to a meal; many are served cold. This chapter offers a number from which to choose.

Snails can't be denied their importance. In the shell or out, they exude Gallic pleasure; with eggs (page 14), they make a surprising showing. (For more first-course egg dishes, see pages 73-74.)

Additionally, you will find directions for serving foods you simply buy and eat. But first, a look at the way vegetables might open a meal.

Assorted vegetable salads

(Assortiment de crudités)

Vegetable salads—those made with ingredients other than lettuce—play a major role as first courses in French dining.

One of the most typical presentations is a colorful offering of "crudités" (raw or cooked vegetables) in a dressing. Usually there are several salads grouped to make up the crudités; you might choose just one or sample them all. If you want to prepare an assortment of crudités, allow a total of ½ to ¾ cup salad for each person.

Often the salads are accompanied by slices of a terrine (pages 11 and 12) or a hard-cooked egg dish, such as whole or half eggs topped with mayonnaise (flavored to taste with mustard or watercress, page 74).

Present the salads in individual dishes grouped on a tray, or mound them onto lettuce leaves. The celery root, radish, beet, carrot, green pepper, artichoke, and cucumber salads all have the advantage of holding well if made several hours ahead and kept cold.

Parsley dressing

(Sauce vinaigrette)

Blend 1 cup **salad oil** or olive oil with ½ cup **wine vinegar** or lemon juice, 3 tablespoons minced **parsley**, 1 tablespoon **Dijon mustard**, ½ teaspoon **salt**, ¼ teaspoon **thyme leaves** (optional), and ¼ teaspoon **pepper**. Stir before each use. (Dressing can be refrigerated until next day; if you want a smaller quantity, though, make up just half the recipe.) Makes about 1¼ cups.

Celery root salad

(Céleri remoulade)

Cut in matchstick-size pieces enough peeled **celery root** (about 1 small root) to make 1 cup. Blend with 3 tablespoons *each* **mayonnaise** and **parsley dressing** (above). **Salt** to taste. Cover and chill if made ahead. Makes about 1 cup.

Radish salad

(Salade de radis)

Thinly slice enough **red radishes** to make 1 cup. Blend with ¼ cup **parsley dressing** (above) and **salt** to taste. Cover and chill if made ahead. Makes about 1 cup.

Marinated beet salad

(Salade de betteraves)

Blend ¼ cup **parsley dressing** (left) with 1 cup cooked diced or julienne **beets** (may be canned). **Salt** to taste. Cover and chill if made ahead. Makes about 1 cup.

Shredded carrot salad

(Carottes râpées)

Peel and finely shred enough **carrots** (about 2) to make 1 cup. Blend with ¼ cup **parsley dressing** (left). Or you can add 2 tablespoons mayonnaise, if desired. **Salt** to taste. Cover and chill if made ahead. Makes about 1 cup.

Green pepper salad

(Salade de poivrons)

Sliver enough **green peppers** (about 1 large—seeds and core removed) to make 1 cup. Mix with 3 tablespoons **parsley dressing** (left) and **salt** to taste. Cover and chill if made ahead. Makes about 1 cup.

Apéritifs: a refreshing way to begin

To precede a meal with a gentle apéritif is quite European—often with much discussion as to the "digestive" properties of the beverage. The most widely favored apéritifs are aromatic wines; these include vermouths and wines that are flavored with herbs and other products and fortified with alcohol.

Many of the wines have the bitter tang of quinine. Europeans living in the tropics helped to popularize these flavored wines when they discovered that quinine (the antidote for malaria) was more palatable when swallowed with some wine. Eventually, quinine-flavored wines became appreciated in their own right for their refreshing bitterness.

Apéritif wines include vermouth (sweet or dry or blends of the two), Byrrh, Lillet, Bonal, St. Raphael, Campari, Chambraise, Dubonnet, and Positano. They may be served straight or over ice —or with ice, soda water, and a lemon twist.

Accompany apéritifs with such snacks as roasted almonds or filberts, olives, pâté and crackers, bread sticks and butter.

Artichokes vinaigrette
(Artichauts vinaigrettes)

You can use fresh cooked, cooked frozen, or drained water-packed artichoke hearts to make this salad mixed with housewife's dressing.

Blend a recipe's worth of **housewife's dressing** (page 71) with 2 cups cooked, drained **artichoke hearts**. **Salt** to taste. Cover and let stand at least 1 hour before serving (or cover and chill as long as 2 days if made ahead).

Garnish, if you like, with sprigs of **watercress** or parsley. Makes 4 servings.

Cucumber salad
(Salade de concombres)

Crème fraîche dressing is made with whipping cream you let "ripen" to a tangy flavor by culturing with buttermilk. Directions for making crème fraîche, an ingredient used throughout this book, are on page 77.

Peel (and core if seeds are coarse) and thinly slice 2 medium-size **cucumbers**. Sprinkle with **salt** and let stand in a colander to drain about 1 hour. Rinse and drain.

Blend in a double recipe's worth of **crème fraîche dressing** (page 71); **salt** to taste. Serve at once (or cover and chill until next day; mix before serving). Makes 4 to 6 servings.

Chicken liver pâté
(Pâté de foies de volailles)

Rare is the French household without a favorite liver-flavored pâté, the best of which achieves a silken texture comparable to costly foie gras. This one is not only quick to make, but ultrasmooth.

Melt ½ cup (¼ lb.) **butter** or margarine in a wide frying pan. Add 1 pound **chicken livers** (cut in halves), ¼ pound chopped **mushrooms**, ¼ cup chopped **parsley**, ¼ cup chopped **shallots** or green onions, and ½ teaspoon *each* **thyme leaves** and **salt**. Cook, stirring often, on medium heat until livers are just firm but slightly pink in center (cut to test).

In a very small pan, warm 2 tablespoons **brandy** or madeira and set aflame (*not beneath an exhaust fan or flammable items*); then pour in with livers and shake pan until flame dies. Add ½ cup **dry**

WAYS TO START A MEAL, from left to right: potted pork (rillettes), country terrine with aspic, chicken liver pâté. Serve one or several with toast and very sour pickles called "cornichons."

red wine; heat to simmering; then let mixture cool to room temperature.

In a blender or food processor, smoothly purée livers with liquid. Then add, in chunks, a total of 1 cup (½ lb.) **butter** or margarine, blending until smooth.

If desired, you can stir in 1 can (about 3/7-oz. size) **black truffle**, thinly sliced or minced, distributing evenly.

Pour mixture into a deep, straight-sided rectangular 4 to 5-cup dish or pan. Cover and chill overnight or up to 1 week; freeze for longer storage. Cut in slices to serve (use a wide spatula to lift out portions; first slice is usually difficult to remove neatly). Present on a plate, to eat with **crusty bread** or toast, accompanied by **sour pickles** (page 13). Makes 12 to 16 servings.

Country terrine with aspic
(Terrine de campagne en gelée)

A terrine is a container (page 7) and also the name given the glorified meat loaf baked in it. Pâté means paste or pastelike; the ground meat base can be called a pâté, or if it is enclosed in a pastry or dough, this, too, can be called a pâté. So the same dish can be called pâté, terrine, or pâté in a terrine. Take your choice of names and how you make the dish—several variations follow.

Traditionally, a terrine is served cold, thickly sliced, as a first course to go with crusty bread or toast and sour pickles (page 13). Often a tender lettuce leaf is placed beneath the slice of meat.

But also consider these tasty cold meat loaves for sandwiches or to serve with salad for a lunch or light supper. They improve in flavor—as the seasonings mingle—after a day or two.

Finely chop 1 small **onion**; cook until soft in 2 tablespoons **butter** or margarine. Add 2 tablespoons **madeira**, sherry, or port and boil dry, stirring; set aside.

Mix together until blended ½ pound *each* **bulk pork sausage** and **ground veal**; 1 **egg**, 2 tablespoons **all-purpose flour**, ¼ cup (from 10½-oz. can) **condensed consommé** (reserve leftover); 1 to 3 cloves **garlic**, minced or pressed; ½ teaspoon *each* **salt** and **thyme leaves**; ¼ teaspoon **ground ginger**, and onion mixture.

Pack meat into a deep, straight-sided 3 to 4-cup pan or baking dish, cover, and set in a pan containing at least 1 inch **scalding water**. Bake in a 350° oven for 1 hour and 10 minutes or until meat has lost its pink color in center (cut a gash to test).

Remove from the oven; skim off and discard as much fat as possible (retaining meat juices); then pour reserved consommé onto meat.

(Continued on next page)

Cover and chill until consommé gels. Store as long as 4 to 5 days in refrigerator. Garnish with 2 or 3 **bay leaves** and **whole black pepper**. To serve, cut in slices and lift from dish. Makes 8 servings.

Wrapped terrine
(Terrine bardée de lard)

The French use a special fat from fresh pork to enclose the ground meat mixture for a terrine; it gives the terrine a tidy, classic look and also adds to its flavor. Readily available, bacon is an alternate for the pork fat; you simmer it briefly before using to minimize the smoked flavor.

Prepare **meat mixture** as directed for country terrine with aspic (preceding recipe), substituting **dry white wine** or whipping cream for the ¼ cup **condensed consommé**, if you like.

Place ½ pound thinly sliced **bacon** in a wide frying pan. Cover with **water** and place on medium heat; when just at simmering, remove from heat, drain, and allow to cool.

Line bottom and sides of a deep, straight-sided 3 to 4-cup pan or baking dish (oval or rectangular) with bacon, allowing slices to extend 2 or 3 inches over rim. Pack meat into bacon-lined dish, then fold extended bacon slices over meat to cover it. Lay 1 or 2 **bay leaves** and 5 or 6 **whole black peppers** on bacon. Bake as directed for country terrine with aspic.

Remove from oven, uncover, and let cool slightly at room temperature. Set terrine in another pan (to catch any juices that might overflow) and place a flat plate, slightly smaller than baking container, on meat (or use heavy cardboard, cut to fit top of container and sealed in foil). Place a weight, such as canned goods, on top to press down surface of terrine; chill thoroughly. (This step compacts meat and flattens curve that develops on surface as meat bakes.) Use within a week or freeze for longer storage.

To serve, cut in slices and lift from container. Or, immerse terrine in very **hot water** up to rim just until a little exterior fat of meat begins to melt (takes only a few seconds) and turn meat out onto a serving dish. Slice to serve (or cover and chill until ready to serve). Makes 8 servings.

Garnishing a terrine
(La garniture d'une terrine)

You can add various things to a terrine as you assemble it, contributing flavor and a decorative pattern when the meat is sliced.

Fill baking container with ⅓ to ½ of **meat mixture** at a time (follow directions for country terrine in aspic or wrapped terrine, preceding), spreading meat smoothly. On each layer, place portions of 1 to 3 of the following:

Whole shelled **pistachios** (may be salted); allow 2 to 3 tablespoons for a terrine.

Chicken or duck livers cut in halves (1 or 2 livers for a terrine); cover livers with **water**, heat just to boiling, drain, and use.

Strips of **cooked meat**, such as tongue (plain, corned, or smoked), ham, duck, or turkey (⅛ to ¼ lb. for a terrine); arrange strips so you will cut across them when you slice terrine. Make strips ¼ to ½ inch wide and as long as baking container.

Cooked sausages in casing, such as pork links, mild Italian, or salsicce vin blanc (allow about ¼ lb. for a terrine).

Sliced or diced **black truffles**; add any truffle juice to meat mixture (use as many truffles as the budget allows—about ½ oz. is generous for a terrine).

Potted pork from Tours
(Rillettes de Tours)

This savory meat spread is considered peasant fare, for it is hearty and robust. Chunks of pork, fat, and seasonings bake long and slowly until the meat literally falls apart. Then you pull it into shreds, mixing with juices and some fat to make a spread.

Rillettes is a bold appetizer served on crusty bread, toast, or crackers; it also makes a great sandwich filling.

If you have a pressure cooker, you may want to try a quick way to make rillettes (directions follow).

Cut 3 pounds **fairly lean, boneless pork** (from shoulder, butt, or loin end) into about 1½-inch chunks and place in a heavy 2-quart casserole.

Mix in 2 teaspoons **salt**; 1 teaspoon **pepper**; 1 clove **garlic**, minced or pressed; ½ teaspoon **thyme leaves**; and 1 **bay leaf**. Add 1 cup **water**. Cut about ½ pound **pork fat** in chunks and lay evenly over meat.

Cover and bake in a 250° oven for about 4 hours or until meat is soft enough to fall apart in shreds when pulled with a fork.

Drain off juices and fat; skim fat from juices and reserve both, separately. Discard bay leaf and any lumps of fat. Break pork into tiny fibers by pulling apart with 2 forks. Blend reserved juices with meat; taste and add **salt** if needed. Pack rillettes compactly into several small crocks or one large one; then pour in enough fat to cover surface in about a ⅛-inch layer. Discard remaining fat. Cover and chill up to 1 week; freeze for longer storage.

Let come to room temperature before serving. At that time, scrape off surface fat and scoop meat out to spread on **crusty bread** or hot toast; it is also good on wide strips of **green or red peppers**, slices of raw turnips, or slices of the large radish—daikon. Makes about 4 cups.

Pressure cooker method. Place **pork**, **salt**, **pepper**, **garlic**, **thyme leaves**, **bay leaf**, and **water** in a 4-quart pressure cooker (without rack); set **pork fat** on top.

Bring cooker to 10 pounds pressure according to manufacturer's directions and cook for 1 hour. Reduce pressure under cold running water; open pan. Pour off juices and fat and separate; reserve both. Shred meat as directed; return juices and add **salt** to taste. Pack compactly into crocks; cover, chill, and serve as directed. Makes about 4 cups.

Fish terrine

(Terrine de poisson)

Like a meat terrine, this delicate ground fish mixture is baked in a casserole surrounded by a water bath that prevents browning and gives a poached quality to the finished dish. It is quite attractive—the slices are white with a pink salmon core. Serve the terrine chilled, with hollandaise.

Melt ¼ cup **butter** or margarine in a frying pan. Add ¼ cup chopped **shallots** or green onion and cook over medium heat, stirring, until soft. Add ½ teaspoon **tarragon leaves** and 2 tablespoons **lemon juice**. Blend in ¼ cup unsifted **all-purpose flour**.

Cornichons: little green pickles

Sometimes you can purchase in fancy food stores the very small and intensely sour pickles called "cornichons." Packed in vinegar with tarragon, they are imported from France and are expensive.

You can make mock cornichons using this modification of tiny sweet gherkins, which are plentiful.

Sour pickles: mock cornichons

Drain and measure liquid from a jar of **tiny sweet gherkins**. Measure an equal amount of **white wine vinegar** and add ½ teaspoon **tarragon leaves** for each 1 to 1½ cups pickles; discard pickle juice.

In a small pan, bring vinegar to boiling; then pour over pickles. Cover and chill at least 24 hours before serving.

Remove from heat and stir in 1½ cups **half-and-half** (light cream) and ½ teaspoon **salt**. Bring to a boil, stirring. Remove from heat and stir in 3 slightly beaten **eggs**.

In a blender or food processor, whirl until smooth ½ pound **small cooked shrimp** and ½ pound **lean, boneless, white-fleshed fish** (such as sole, Greenland turbot, or halibut), adding cooked sauce as needed to liquefy. Stir in remaining sauce.

Pour half the mixture into a deep, straight-sided 6-cup terrine or 5 by 7-inch loaf pan. Cut a ½-pound boned and skinned **salmon fillet** into 1-inch-wide lengths and distribute evenly down center of casserole. Top with remaining puréed fish. Cover dish and set in a larger container filled with **scalding water** to about half the depth of fish-filled dish.

Bake in a 350° oven for 30 minutes or until firm. Remove from oven, cover, and chill.

Cut terrine in thick slices in container and support with a wide spatula to lift out portions. Serve slices on **butter lettuce leaves**. Accompany with **hollandaise** or béarnaise (pages 69-70), allowing 2 or 3 tablespoons for each serving. Makes 8 to 10 servings.

Naturals

Some of the most appealing foods you might serve as a first course require virtually no effort to present.

Smoked salmon—Garnish with slices of **onion**, whole **capers**, and **lemon wedges** to go with **toast** and **butter**. Two or 3 salmon slices make a serving.

Oysters on the half shell—Accompany with **prepared horseradish**, **lemon wedges**, and a **cocktail sauce**. Allow 4 to 6 oysters for a serving.

Caviar—Serve icy cold to spoon onto **toast**, with garnishes of minced **onion**, finely chopped **hard-cooked egg**, **sour cream**, and **lemon wedges**. You can serve elegant caviar of sturgeon; or refresh the crunchy, appealing caviar of lumpfish or whitefish by placing it in a fine wire strainer and rinsing under cold running water; then drain well and chill. Plan on 1 or 2 tablespoons caviar for a serving.

Cold meats—Serve thinly sliced, such as one might purchase in a charcuterie (delicatessen) in France; consider specially **cured ham** like prosciutto (jambon cru de pays), **dry sausages** like salami (saucisson), or **moist sausages** like galantina or mortadella. A few slices (about ⅛ pound) on a plate to eat with knife and fork make a serving.

Ripe crescents of golden melon—A perfectly ripe **cantaloupe** is most like the hard-shelled, golden-fleshed melon common in France. Other melons—honeydew, Crenshaw, casaba, Persian—are also elegant meal starters. Serve a melon slice plain, with **lemon wedges**, or even with a few thin slices of **prosciutto** to make a serving.

Herring salads—In great variety from plain to creamy, these are surprisingly commonplace in France. You can serve chilled herring salad (purchased or homemade) on **lettuce leaves** to eat with knife and fork, accompanied by **crusty bread**. Plan about ¼ to ½ cup herring for a serving.

Cold, cooked shellfish—Shrimp, crab, or lobster may be accompanied by **mayonnaise** (page 69) or watercress mayonnaise (page 69) or with a dressing such as parsley dressing (page 9). Allow 2 to 3 ounces for a serving.

Snails with herb butter
(Escargots à la bourguignonne)

Canned snails are a fine delicacy to keep on hand for occasions that call for a smashing appetizer. Snails are sold with or without the natural, reusable shells; other shell containers are the ceramic snail shells available in specialty cookware shops.

Additional accessories for snails served in the shells are the pans or dishes with individual cups for the shells, snail clamps to hold the shells steady as you eat, and snail forks (page 7).

Drain 1 can of 24-count large **cooked snails**; then rinse under cold water and drain well.

To make herb butter, mix together ½ cup (¼ lb.) **butter** or margarine; 2 small cloves **garlic**, minced or pressed; 2 teaspoons minced **chives**, shallots, or green onion (with some tops); and 2 tablespoons minced **parsley**.

Put a bit of butter in each of 24 clean, dry snail shells; then tuck in a snail. Seal snails in with remaining butter, using all. Press buttered surface in grated **Parmesan cheese** (6 to 8 tablespoons total).

Arrange shells, cheese side up, in 4 small pans (6-snail size) or 4 individual baking pans. (If made ahead, cover and chill until ready to cook.)

Bake, uncovered, in a 500° oven for 7 minutes or until cheese is lightly browned and butter is bubbling. Serve with **French bread** or rolls to soak up garlic butter. Makes 4 servings of 6 snails each.

Eggs with snails on toast
(Oeufs aux escargots sur canapés)

Swiss-cheese-cloaked escargots, out of the shell and perched on herb-buttered toast, are an elegant complement for scrambled eggs.

Trim crusts from 6 slices **firm-textured white bread** to make neat rectangles. Cut each slice in quarters and place on a baking sheet. Bake in a 350° oven for about 12 to 15 minutes or until lightly toasted.

Spread one side of each piece of toast with **herb butter** (see snails with herb butter, preceding), using about half the butter. Drain 1 can of 24-count large **cooked snails**; then rinse under cold water and drain well. Top each toast with a snail. Dot snails with remaining butter; then sprinkle evenly with about ¼ cup shredded **Swiss cheese**.

Return to a 350° oven until cheese melts (about 3 minutes). Keep warm (oven off and door ajar) while you cook eggs. Put 4 serving plates in oven to warm.

In a large frying pan, melt 2 tablespoons **butter** or margarine over low heat; then add 8 slightly beaten **eggs**. As they cook, gently push the mixture from pan bottom, allowing uncooked portion to flow down from surface; cook until as set as you like.

Spoon eggs equally onto warm serving plates. Set 6 prepared toast pieces around each serving of eggs. Sprinkle eggs with a total of 2 or 3 tablespoons chopped **chives** or green onion (including some tops) and **salt** to taste. Makes 4 servings.

Provençal anchovy sauce
(Anchoiade provençale)

In the south of France, this pungent sauce is served to spread on bread, or it may be presented as a dip or spread for raw or cooked vegetables, hard-cooked eggs, or cold cooked fish. It makes a handsome and hearty appetizer to serve before a light supper—perhaps a soup meal. Or you might make it as a main course for lunch to serve 6 to 8.

In a blender or food processor, combine 3 cans (2 oz. *each*) well-drained **anchovy fillets** and ¼ cup **red wine vinegar**; whirl until puréed. Add ¾ cup **olive oil**, ½ cup packed **parsley**, 4 cloves **garlic**, and ¼ teaspoon **pepper**; whirl until blended. Cover and chill at least several hours or until next day. Makes 2 cups sauce, or dip for 12 to 16 servings.

Foods to serve with anchovy sauce. You'll need about 6 to 8 cups vegetables. Choose 2 or 3 kinds of **raw vegetables** such as celery, cucumbers, green onions, radishes, or whole mushrooms, and 1 or 2 cold **cooked vegetables** such as green beans, asparagus, or artichokes. If you like, include 4 to 6 quartered **hard-cooked eggs** and 1 to 1½ pounds cold, cooked, shelled and deveined **shrimp** (medium or large) or cold cooked halibut, cut in cubes. Offer sliced **French bread**, too.

Warming soups

"Cooking in the fireplace adds to the flavor of a meal as well as the food."

Perhaps soups best demonstrate one important aspect of French cuisine: the sophistication of a knowing simplicity.

Even in this brief collection of vegetable soups, deceptively simple ingredients, though few, are balanced wisely in order to create a specific taste.

Mushrooms are more mushroomy when mellowed by gently sautéed onions; peas are sweeter when tempered by a bit of carrot; leeks seem smoother, richer when potatoes add quiet body; onions show off best in a rich, meaty broth that is seasoned by other vegetables. On down the list of the soups, one vegetable helps another achieve unexpected potential.

One of the finest tools in making good soup is good broth. You can get by passably with canned broth, but there is much to be said for making your own. First, it's a practical step—bones and scraps that might have no other use are put to work. Second, the broth (as detailed on page 16) provides a running start for quality in any soup and is even delicious in its own right.

These soups are to serve, as in France, when a meal begins; in the evening, hot soup is the choice more often than cold, simply because its warmth is welcome as the day cools. If there is an hors d'oeuvre, such as from the preceding chapter, it will typically precede the soup.

Generous portions of any of these soups can be considered as a light main dish to go with cold meats, sandwiches, or a meaty hors d'oeuvre. For whole-meal fish soups, see page 30.

Homemade broth for a multitude of uses

Thanks to freezers, it's easy to accumulate a variety of scraps and bones that are excellent for making broth.

Rich meat broth

(Consommé)

Assemble 12 to 14 pounds **bones** and **scraps** (cooked or raw, or a combination) from chicken, turkey, duck (plus any poultry skin or giblets, except livers), lamb, pork, ham, or beef (limit bare beef bones to about 1/3 of total). A mixture of meats gives best flavor. If pieces are large, cut or break them so they fit compactly in a kettle at least 10-quart size (larger is better); this amount should fill kettle to about 6-quart level.

Spread meat and bones out in a large rimmed baking pan. Bake at 400° for 1 hour and 15 minutes or until bones and scraps are well browned. When cool enough to handle, transfer meat and all drippings to kettle. With a little **water**, rinse all browned bits from baking pan and add this liquid to kettle.

Add 4 to 5 *each* medium-size **onions** and **carrots**, cut in chunks; 1 medium-size **turnip**, cut in chunks; 8 to 10 **parsley** sprigs; 10 to 12 **whole black peppers**; and 2 **bay leaves**. Then pour in 5 quarts **water**; it should cover other ingredients.

Bring liquid to a boil, cover, and boil slowly for about 4 hours. Let stand until fairly cool, then lift out and discard most big bones. Pour broth and small bones into a colander, catching broth in another container. To remove tiny scraps, next pour broth through a colander lined with a moistened cloth.

Chill broth; lift off and discard all fat. Heat broth slightly to liquefy; then measure—if you have more than 3 quarts broth, boil rapidly to reduce to this amount; if less than 3 quarts, add **water** to make this volume. *Do not salt broth* because if you concentrate (or reduce) broth later, it can become too salty. Salt to taste when ready to use.

Refrigerate as long as a week or freeze (in small, usable portions such as 1 or 2 cups) for longer storage. Makes 3 quarts.

Serve as a soup

Rich meat broth makes an elegant soup if only heated and salted to taste. If you want sparkling clear broth, you need to clarify it according to the following steps:

Clarifying broth. For each 4 cups broth, you will need 2 **egg whites**. Bring broth to a rolling boil. Beat egg whites until foamy, then whip into boiling broth. Return to a full boil, remove from heat, and let stand until slightly cooled.

Moisten a muslin cloth with **cold water**, wring dry and use it to line a wire strainer placed over a large container. Pour broth through cloth without flooding—egg whites slow the draining. Draw up cloth into a bag and gently squeeze out as much liquid as possible; discard whites. For broth of exceptional clarity, repeat steps.

Simple embellishments. To serve as a soup, consider these simple additions for broth:

Cut cold **French pancakes** (page 81) into thin strips and sprinkle 2 or 3 tablespoons of these into each serving of steaming rich meat broth.

Stir 1 tablespoon **sherry**, madeira, or port into each serving of hot rich meat broth.

Cut **marrow** (page 61) into bite-size pieces and add 4 to 5 pieces to each serving of hot rich meat broth.

Pass shredded **Gruyère**, Swiss, or Parmesan cheese to spoon into servings of hot rich meat broth.

Add buttered **plain or seasoned croutons**, along with **cheese** (preceding) to servings of hot rich meat broth.

Meat glaze

(Glace de viande)

Greatly concentrated broth makes this intensely flavored sauce which you can use to flavor stews, soups, sauces, vegetables. Add meat glaze by the spoonful to achieve the flavor desired; it is the tasty homemade version of bottled meat extract.

In a wide pan boil rapidly 4 cups **rich meat broth** (preceding) until it is thick enough to make a shiny velvety coating on a spoon—large shiny bubbles also form in boiling broth; you will have about 1/3 cup.

Store meat glaze, covered, in refrigerator as long as 1 week; freeze for longer storage. Because sauce is rubbery when cooled, you can cut chilled glaze in cubes and freeze, then package; take desired quantity from freezer as needed. Glaze melts quickly when heated. Makes about 1/3 cup.

Green pea soup

(Potage Saint-Germain)

Carrots give the sweetness, tender tiny peas (such as are available frozen) add the color to the smooth puréed soup. It's a good example of how thoughtfully matched flavors can create the impression of richness without excessive calories—something the French do exceptionally well.

        1 **can (about 14 oz.) regular-strength chicken broth or 2 cups rich meat broth (page 16)**
        1 **medium-size carrot, diced**
        1 **teaspoon chervil leaves or 1 tablespoon chopped parsley**
        1 **package (10 oz.) frozen petite peas, thawed**
        2 **tablespoons butter or margarine**
           Salt and pepper

In a 2 to 3-quart pan, bring to a boil broth, carrot, and chervil. Reduce heat and simmer, covered, 10 minutes or until carrots are tender. Whirl broth and peas in a blender or food processor, a portion at a time, until smooth (or force through a food mill or wire strainer). Return to pan, stir in butter, and heat through. (Chill until next day if made ahead; reheat or serve cold.) Makes about 1 quart or 4 to 5 servings of 1-cup size.

Cream of mushroom soup

(Crème de champignons)

Mushroom purée, with a bright sprinkling of parsley, can be the mild but well-stated starting point for a meal featuring a highly seasoned main dish, such as steak with green peppercorn sauce (page 61).

"In the evening the warm soup is most welcome."

Slice ½ pound **mushrooms**, chop 1 medium-size **onion**, and chop 1 cup lightly packed **parsley**. Sauté vegetables, uncovered, in ¼ cup melted **butter** or margarine in a frying pan over high heat, stirring, until mushrooms are limp and all juices have evaporated.

Stir in 1 tablespoon **all-purpose flour**; remove from heat and blend in 1 can (14 oz.) **regular-strength beef broth** or 2 cups rich meat broth (page 16). Bring to a boil, stirring.

Whirl mixture with 1 cup **sour cream** or crème fraîche (page 77), a portion at a time, in a blender or food processor until smooth (or force through a food mill or wire strainer). If made ahead, cover and chill until next day; reheat to serve. Makes about 1 quart or 4 to 5 servings of 1-cup size.

Onion soup

(Soupe à l'oignon gratinée)

Onion soup, as was served to working men in the now defunct Les Halles of Paris, is one of the world's celebrated soups. Toast—encrusted on top with melted cheese, saturated beneath by the richly flavored, onion-laced broth—distinguishes this substantial soup. It can serve as a light entrée after a slice of meaty terrine.

There are sharable secrets for making good onion soup; sauté the onions very slowly until they take on a rich caramel color; use a good-tasting broth; and serve in individual bowls so each portion has its own baked-on topping.

        6 **large onions, thinly sliced**
        1 **tablespoon olive oil**
        4 **tablespoons butter or margarine**
        6 **cups regular-strength beef broth or rich meat broth (page 16)**
           Salt and pepper
        ⅓ **cup port**
        ½ **cup diced Gruyère or Swiss cheese**
           Dry-toasted French bread (directions follow)
        ½ **cup shredded Gruyère or Swiss cheese**
        ½ **cup shredded Parmesan cheese**

In a 3 to 4-quart pan on medium-low heat, cook onions slowly, uncovered, in olive oil and 2 tablespoons of the butter until limp and caramel colored but not browned (takes about 40 minutes). Add broth and bring to a boil. Reduce heat, cover, and simmer for 30 minutes. Season to taste with salt and pepper and stir in port. (If made ahead cover and chill until next day. Reheat to continue.)

Pour into 6 individual oven-proof soup bowls. Sprinkle equal amounts of diced Gruyère cheese into each bowl and set a piece of toast on top. Sprinkle equally with shredded Gruyère and Parmesan. Melt remaining 2 tablespoons butter. Drizzle evenly over toast.

(Continued on page 19)

Place soup in a 425° oven for 10 minutes; then broil about 4 inches from heat just until cheese browns lightly on top. Makes 6 servings of 1½ to 2-cup size.

Dry-toasted French bread. Cut 6 slices French bread, each ½ inch thick. Place on a baking sheet in a 325° oven for 20 to 25 minutes or until lightly toasted. (Wrap airtight if made ahead.) Spread each slice with butter or margarine.

Vegetable soup
(Potage de légumes)

Golden with carrots, this vegetable soup is thickened by vegetables that also include potato, turnip, onion, and leek. Embellish each smooth serving with a generous dollop of cream.

In a 3 or 4-quart pan, melt 2 tablespoons **butter** or margarine. Add 1 large **onion**, chopped, and 1 sliced **leek** (white part only); cook, stirring, until soft. Pour in 3 cans (about 14 oz. *each*) **regular-strength chicken broth** or 6 cups rich meat broth (page 16); set off heat.

Peel and dice 1 medium-size **potato**, 1 medium-size **turnip**, and 8 medium-size **carrots**; add to broth along with ¼ teaspoon **thyme leaves**. Bring broth to a boil; reduce heat, cover, and simmer about 20 minutes or until vegetables are soft enough to mash easily.

In a blender or food processor, whirl, a portion at a time, until smooth (or force through a food mill or wire strainer).

Return soup to pan, add **salt** to taste, and, if desired, thin with additional broth (soup is typically very thick); heat to simmering. (Or chill, covered; then serve cold or reheat.) Ladle into bowls and, if you like, add spoonfuls of **whipping cream**, sour cream, or crème fraîche (page 77) to each serving. Makes about 2 quarts or 7 to 8 servings of 1-cup size.

Tomato soup
(Soupe aux tomates)

Fresh tomato flavor is achieved with just one ripe tomato. Added last for texture and color, it refreshes a sweet blend of canned tomato purée and puréed onion. Finishing touches at the table are toppings of cheese, crème fraîche, and crusty seasoned croutons.

FOUR QUICK-TO-COOK SOUPS make use of 11 different vegetables to achieve their fresh and wholesome taste: green watercress soup, white cauliflower soup, golden vegetable soup (dominated by carrots), and red tomato soup.

In a blender or food processor, whirl until smooth (or force through a food mill or wire strainer) 3 tablespoons melted **butter** or margarine, 1 medium-size **onion**, cut in chunks, and 1 can (6 oz.) **tomato paste**.

Pour into a 3 to 4-quart pan and cook over medium heat, stirring, until boiling vigorously.

Add 2 cans (about 14 oz. *each*) **regular-strength chicken broth** or 4 cups rich meat broth (page 16) and 1 large **tomato**, finely chopped (include juices). Heat to simmering, **salt** to taste, and serve. (Or cover, chill until next day, and reheat.)

Ladle into serving bowls. Pass shredded **Gruyère cheese** or Swiss cheese, **sour cream** or crème fraîche (page 77), and **seasoned croutons** to add to soup according to taste. You'll need about 1 cup of each. Makes about 1 quart or 4 to 5 servings of 1-cup size.

Cauliflower soup
(Potage Dubarry)

Swirl a pat of golden butter into each serving of cauliflower soup just before it's presented; then dust with ground nutmeg.

In a 3 to 4-quart pan combine 2 cans (about 14 oz. *each*) **regular-strength chicken broth** or 4 cups rich meat broth (page 16), 1 medium-size (about 1 lb.) **cauliflower**, thinly sliced, and 2 thinly sliced **leeks** (white part only). Bring to a boil, cover, and simmer for about 15 minutes or until cauliflower is tender enough to mash easily.

In a blender or food processor, whirl mixture, a portion at a time, until smooth (or force through a food mill or wire strainer). Return to pan, add 1 cup **whipping cream**, ¼ teaspoon **ground nutmeg**, and **salt** to taste; heat to simmering. (Or chill, covered, until next day; then reheat to serve.)

Ladle into bowls and, if desired, add to each a small lump of **butter**; then sprinkle with more **ground nutmeg**. Makes about 1½ quarts or 5 to 6 servings of 1-cup size.

Watercress soup
(Potage au cresson)

Bright green watercress soup is an accomplishment. Ordinarily, watercress soup is drab and grayish because heat destroys the color of this vegetable. But if you take the extra step of blanching and chilling the cress, as prescribed here, before adding it to the soup, the brilliance is retained with no loss of flavor.

In a pan (about 3-qt. size), bring to a boil 5 cups **regular-strength chicken broth** or rich meat broth (page 16). Add 1 medium-size **potato**, peeled and coarsely chopped, and 2 medium-size **onions**, coarsely chopped. Cover and simmer for about 20 minutes or until potatoes mash easily.

Measure 1 cup firmly packed **watercress** leaves and stems. Immerse greens in **boiling water**; then drain at once. Immerse in **ice water** just long enough to chill; then drain again.

In a blender or food processor, whirl until smooth, a portion at a time, potato mixture and watercress (or force through a food mill or wire strainer). Return to pan and heat to simmering. (Or cover and chill until next day; then reheat.)

Taste and add **salt**, if desired. Stir in 2 to 4 tablespoons **whipping cream** or crème fraîche (page 77). Ladle into bowls and garnish with additional **watercress** sprigs. Makes about 1½ quarts or 5 to 6 servings of 1-cup size.

Provençal vegetable soup with basil
(*Soupe au pistou*)

"Pistou" is the name of a basil sauce flavoring this soup; it is similar to the Italian pesto sauce.

Shredded cheese, added a little at a time to the hot soup, forms soft, chewy ribbons; but if you add the cheese too quickly, it tends to stay in a big, hard-to-serve lump.

Plan on large portions to start a meal; then follow with cold sliced meat or an omelet.

    2 quarts water or rich meat broth (page 16)
    2 large tomatoes, peeled and coarsely chopped
    1 pound green beans (strings and ends
         removed), cut in 1-inch lengths
    3 medium-size potatoes, peeled and cut into
         ½-inch cubes
       Salt
    ⅛ teaspoon pepper
    ¼ pound vermicelli, broken in short lengths
       Pistou mixture (directions follow)
    1½ cups shredded Swiss cheese

In a pan (about 4-qt. size) bring water to a boil; add tomatoes and their juices, green beans, potatoes, 1 teaspoon salt, and pepper. Cover and simmer 1 hour over low heat. Add vermicelli and cook 15 minutes or until tender. Add more salt, if needed. (This can be done ahead, soup chilled until next day, then reheated.)

Put pistou mixture in a tureen (about 3-qt. size) and pour in hot soup. Gradually stir in ¾ cup of the cheese, adding 2 tablespoons at a time and mixing well after each addition. Serve at once. Pass remaining cheese to be added to taste. Makes about 3 quarts or 6 to 8 servings of 2-cup size.

Pistou mixture. Blend together ½ cup **basil leaves**, 4 cloves **garlic**, minced or pressed, and ¼ cup **olive oil**, mixing to coat basil thoroughly with oil.

Leek soup
(*Soupe aux poireaux*)

Potatoes lend thickness and body to delicately flavored leek soup. Serve it hot and call it "soupe aux poireaux," or cold and call it "vichyssoise."

    4 cups sliced leeks (white part only)
    3 cups diced, peeled potatoes
    6 cups regular-strength chicken broth or
         rich meat broth (page 16)
    1 cup whipping cream or crème fraîche
         (page 77)
    3 tablespoons dry vermouth or sherry
       Salt
       Chopped chives

In a pan (about 3 qt.), combine leeks, potatoes, and broth. Bring to a boil; reduce heat, cover, and simmer until vegetables are soft (about 20 minutes). Whirl mixture, a portion at a time, in a blender or food processor until smooth (or force through a food mill or wire strainer). Return soup to pan, blend in cream and vermouth. Salt to taste.

Sprinkle with chives and serve hot or cold. Makes about 2½ quarts—8 to 10 servings of 1-cup size, 4 to 5 servings of 2-cup size.

Petite marmite
(*Petite marmite*)

Petite marmite has two meanings—it translates to describe a dish of a particular shape—"little kettle"—which is a deep sort of soup bowl in which you can cook, too. It also describes a type of meat-and-broth soup that is commonly cooked and served in this container. Needless to say, any bowls will suffice for serving, and other utensils will do for the cooking.

In a kettle (at least 8-qt. size), combine 8 cups **regular-strength beef broth** or rich meat broth (page 16) with 8 cups **water** (or use all meat broth), 2½ to 3 pounds **lean beef brisket**, and 1 teaspoon **salt**. Bring to a boil; reduce heat, cover, and simmer about 3 hours or until brisket pierces easily.

Add 8 **chicken wings** and simmer 30 minutes. Lift meats from broth and chill, covered. Chill broth; lift off and discard fat when hard.

Return broth to heat, add 2 sliced **carrots** and 2 small sliced **turnips**; cover and simmer about 10 minutes. Cut brisket in bite-size pieces. Add meat and chicken wings to stock. (At this point you can chill, covered, until next day.)

Heat through, covered; **salt** to taste and serve. Pass shredded **Parmesan cheese** to add to each serving. Makes about 4 quarts—16 servings of about 1-cup size or 8 servings of about 2-cup size.

Fish and shellfish

"The best way to begin is with fresh fish from the sea."

The French approach to fish is a good study in opposites. This food with its delicate nature is often seasoned with gentle restraint so the basic flavor is not overburdened. Favorite partners are wine, cream, butter, lemon, shallots, and parsley, as well as herbs added with a sparing hand; these subtle ingredients are combined with many shifts in proportions or numbers, creating a surprising range of experiences, from frankly rich and lavish as for sole veronique to the lean and tasteful austerity of perfectly poached piece of salmon.

By contrast, the French also use the same fish as foils for truly bold flavors: bouillabaisse gets its land-and-sea harmony from the earthy zest of saffron; scallops, clams, and shrimp all take well to bold garlic in some of the regionally styled dishes.

You will find these fish dishes balanced between those that are quickly cooked, those you can prepare ahead, and those whose preparation involves many advance steps. Quenelles and salmon in brioche have to be counted as real culinary productions, but there are lots of places where you can stop and catch your breath.

Additionally, there is a practical aspect to these recipes; when possible, more than one fish is suggested, so that you may shop for best value. The one lobster dish makes the most of cooking showmanship, using eggs as the delicious extender for this costly shellfish.

Fish dumplings

(Quenelles)

Quenelles—made of a fragile and feathery light fish mixture shaped into ovals or cylinders—are poached in water to firm, then served with a shrimp sauce that is flavored by the shrimp shells.

Quenelles may be a first course or an entreé. They can be started ahead, but are best served freshly cooked. The nantua sauce can be made early and reheated.

A well-made quenelle is one measure of a cook's skill. The goal is to make dumplings as tender as possible that will not fall apart when cooked. Gentle handling is imperative.

In a food processor or food chopper (with fine blade), grind about 1 pound **boneless, skinned halibut** (or other lean whitefish) and 1 pound shelled and deveined **shrimp** (reserve shells for nantua sauce; recipe follows).

In a pan, heat ¾ cup **milk** with ¼ teaspoon **salt** and 2 tablespoons **butter** or margarine, stirring until butter melts. At once add ½ cup plus 2 tablespoons unsifted **all-purpose flour** and stir vigorously on medium heat until dough forms a smooth ball in pan.

Remove from heat and beat in 2 **eggs**, one at a time. Let cool, stirring occasionally. Stir in ground fish, 2 additional tablespoons room-temperature **butter** or margarine, 1 **egg white**, **salt** to taste, and ⅛ teaspoon **white pepper**. Beat until blended; then cover and chill.

Have ready a wide, deep (at least 2 inches) frying pan, well-buttered. To shape quenelles, scoop up with wet hands ¼-cup-size portions of quenelle mixture. Form into smooth egg shapes (about 2½ inches long); then carefully lay into frying pan. Repeat to shape each quenelle and place slightly apart from others. Do not stack. (Shaped quenelles can be covered and chilled up to 4 hours.)

Carefully pour down side of pan enough **boiling water** (about 6 cups) to cover quenelles. (Do not pour over quenelles—it breaks them apart.) Add 2 teaspoons **salt**. Place on very low heat (water should never jiggle or boil) and cook about 15 minutes; turn gently after 8 minutes. Lift quenelles from water with a slotted spoon, drain, and place side by side in a shallow serving dish. Spoon hot **nantua sauce** (recipe follows) over quenelles and serve at once. Makes 16 quenelles—8 first-course servings or 4 main-dish servings.

Nantua sauce. In a small pan, bring to a boil ¾ cup *each* **water** and **dry white wine** with 1 **lemon** slice and 3 or 4 **onion** slices; cover and simmer 5 minutes. Add ¾ pound **shrimp** and cook, uncovered, over medium heat for about 5 minutes or until shrimp are bright pink. Let shrimp cool in liquid.

Remove shrimp; reserve broth and discard onion and lemon. Shell and devein shrimp and set aside, saving shells. Place shells and reserved shells from quenelles in a pan with 2 tablespoons **butter** or margarine and cook over low heat for about 5 minutes, mashing shells with a spoon as they simmer. Add 2 tablespoons warm **brandy** and set aflame (*not beneath an exhaust fan or flammable items*), shaking pan until flames die. Add shrimp liquid and boil until reduced to 1 cup. Strain and reserve liquid; discard shells. Return liquid to pan. Add 1 cup **whipping cream** and boil until reduced to 1½ cups. Blend 1 tablespoon **water** with 2 teaspoons **cornstarch**. Add to cream, stirring over high heat until thickened. Chop shrimp and add to sauce; serve hot. Or cover and chill; to serve, reheat just to simmering.

Sole with shallots in cream

(Sole bonne femme)

Shallots and mushrooms flavor poached sole fillets in this popular home-style dish credited to the "good wife"—bonne femme.

In a wide frying pan, spread ¼ cup minced **shallots**, 2 teaspoons minced **parsley**, and ¼ pound sliced **mushrooms**. Lay 1 pound **sole fillets** on top of mixture, overlapping as little as possible. Pour in ½ cup **dry white wine** (liquid will not cover fillets).

Cover and bring to a boil. Reduce heat and simmer gently for 3 to 5 minutes or until fish turns opaque and flakes easily when prodded with a fork.

With a wide spatula, carefully transfer fillets to a hot serving dish and keep warm. Add **salt** and **pepper** to taste.

Add 1 cup **whipping cream** to frying pan and boil rapidly until sauce is reduced to about ¾ cup and takes on a pale golden color (watch carefully; sauce scorches if reduced too much). Pour evenly over fillets; garnish with **parsley** sprigs and **tomato** wedges. Makes 3 to 4 servings.

Sole curry

(Sole le duc)

Fillet of sole, cut in thin strips, is quickly sautéed. Curry colors and seasons the creamy sauce; green peppercorns give a bitey accent.

Cut 2 pounds **sole fillets** crosswise into 1½-inch-wide strips.

In a wide frying pan, melt ¼ cup **butter** or margarine; add 3 tablespoons minced **shallots** or

CHEESE-DRENCHED SOLE GRATIN *with mushrooms is convenient entrée as it can be assembled day before, then heated in just a few minutes.*

green onion and ¾ teaspoon **curry powder**. Add sole and cook, uncovered, on high heat for about 3 to 5 minutes, shaking pan or pushing fish with a wide spatula to turn; take care not to break up fish. When fish becomes firm and flakes easily when prodded with a fork, gently lift from pan to a serving dish. (At this point, both fish and pan can be set aside and chilled until next day.)

Measure 1 tablespoon canned **green peppercorns** into a strainer, rinse with **cold water**, and drain. Add peppercorns, 1 tablespoon **lemon juice**, and 1 cup **crème fraîche** (page 77) or whipping cream to pan. Boil on high heat, stirring, until big shiny bubbles form (about 6 to 8 minutes); drain any juice from cooked fish into pan. Return fish to sauce, shaking gently to mix with sauce, and heat. Makes 5 or 6 servings.

Sole gratin with mushrooms

(Sole gratinée aux champignons)

Elegant, simple, and make-ahead—three excellent reasons why this is a good dish for entertaining.

First you bake the fish, then use the cooking liquid to make a sauce; both fish and sauce are chilled before combining. When assembled, ready to bake, the dish can be refrigerated overnight. It cooks just long enough to heat through.

Sole would be the first choice of a French cook, but other, more economical fish choices can be made—Greenland turbot, lingcod, halibut, haddock, and sea bass are fine alternatives. Accompany with a green vegetable such as green beans, asparagus, spinach, or broccoli to share sauce.

Arrange about 1½ to 2 pounds **sole fillets** (or other skinned fillets or steaks no thicker than 1 inch) side by side in a shallow casserole so fish is no less than ½ inch thick and no more than 1 inch thick. It may be necessary to fold some fillets in half to make them thick enough. Container size required will vary from 2 to 3 quarts, depending on shape of fish.

Pour into casserole ½ cup **dry white wine** and 1 tablespoon **lemon juice**; sprinkle fish lightly with **salt**. Cover and bake in a 400° oven 10 to 20 minutes, depending upon thickness, or until fish flakes when prodded with a fork in thickest portion.

(Continued on next page)

Drain or siphon off juices and measure. If you have less than 1 cup, add **water** to make this total. If you have more than 1 cup, boil until reduced to this amount; quantity of liquid yielded varies from fish to fish. Cover and chill fish; reserve liquid.

In a wide frying pan, melt 2 tablespoons **butter** or margarine. Add ½ pound sliced **mushrooms** (if you like, leave 3 or 4 mushrooms whole and reserve for garnish) and 1 tablespoon **lemon juice**. Cook, uncovered, on high heat, stirring, until mushrooms are limp and juices have evaporated. Lift out mushrooms and set aside.

Melt 2 more tablespoons **butter** or margarine in pan and stir in 3 tablespoons **all-purpose flour**, stirring until bubbling. Remove from heat and gradually, smoothly, stir in 1 cup reserved fish broth, ½ cup **half-and-half** (light cream) or milk, and ⅛ teaspoon **ground nutmeg**. Return to heat and stir until boiling and thickened. Cover and chill.

Spoon sauce evenly over cold fish. Scatter with ¾ cup shredded **Swiss cheese** or Gruyère cheese and top with whole mushrooms reserved for garnish. (Dish can be covered and chilled until next day.)

Bake, uncovered, in a 400° oven 10 to 15 minutes or until bubbling and cheese is lightly browned. Sprinkle with **ground nutmeg** and serve. Makes 4 to 6 servings.

Fish with sorrel

(Poisson à l'oseille)

Leafy sorrel (see page 69 for how to grow) is a vegetable the French like to use with fish because of its tangy flavor. You can choose from among several kinds of fish for this recipe, either fillets or steaks.

Cut into serving-size pieces 1½ to 2 pounds **boneless, skinned fillets** or steaks (1 inch thick) of salmon, sole, turbot, Greenland turbot, halibut, or other lean, delicately flavored fish. If fish pieces are less than ½ inch thick (such as sole), fold in half.

Melt 2 tablespoons **butter** or margarine in a wide frying pan over medium heat. Arrange fish in an even layer in pan. Sprinkle with ¼ cup minced **shallots** or green onion and 3 tablespoons **lemon juice**. Pour in 1 bottle (8 oz.) **clam juice**. Cover and bring to a boil; then reduce heat and simmer until fish flakes when prodded with a fork (about 5 minutes for fish less than 1 inch thick, about 7 to 8 minutes for fish 1 to 1½ inches thick).

With a wide spatula, transfer fish to a serving platter and keep hot.

Boil fish broth rapidly over high heat until reduced to ¾ cup. Pour into a container and set aside.

In same frying pan, melt 2 tablespoons **butter** or margarine and blend in 2 tablespoons **all-purpose flour**; stir until bubbling. Remove from heat and gradually, smoothly, blend in fish broth, ⅔ cup **half-and-half** (light cream) or milk, 2 tablespoons **lemon juice**, ½ teaspoon **Dijon mustard**, and ⅛ teaspoon **ground nutmeg**; cook, stirring, until boiling and thickened. Stir in 3 cups finely chopped **sorrel** and pour at once over fish; or pour on only enough sauce to coat fish, then pass remaining sauce to add individually. (Sorrel turns a drab color quickly, so serve at once.)

Garnish, if you like, with an additional ½ cup chopped **sorrel** or 2 tablespoons chopped parsley. Makes 4 to 6 servings.

Sole with grapes

(Sole veronique)

Green grapes, heated just long enough to become bright, glistening jewels, are the handsome and delicious accessory for this simple version of a sole classic. Sometimes the fish is poached; here it is sautéed.

Coat 4 to 6 medium-size **sole fillets** (1 to 1½ lb.) with **all-purpose flour**; shake off excess. Sprinkle each fillet lightly with **salt** and **ground nutmeg**.

Melt 2 tablespoons **butter** or margarine in a wide frying pan over medium-high heat. Add fillets and cook until a rich golden color on each side; do not crowd pan (cook fillets in sequence, if necessary). Add 1 more tablespoon **butter**, if needed. Transfer fillets to a serving dish and keep hot.

Add 1 cup **seedless grapes** to pan and swirl about over high heat just until grapes are warm and turn a brighter green. Pour over fish.

Stir into pan ½ cup **whipping cream** and boil on high heat, stirring, until a light golden color; drizzle sauce over fish and serve at once. Makes 4 servings.

Trout with butter sauce

(Truite à la meunière)

The fresher the trout, the more exceptional this simple dish seems. The fish literally swims in lemon juice and melted butter. You can cook fish steaks or fillets in the same manner; fish "à la meunière" is found throughout France and here, too.

Allow 1 or 2 medium-size **trout** (about ½ lb. *each*) per serving. Clean fish, leaving on head and tail; rinse fish and pat dry. Coat fish with **all-purpose flour**; shake off excess.

You can cook about 4 trout at a time in a wide frying pan or fish sauté pan (page 7); if you have more fish, cook them in sequence.

For each 4 fish, melt 2 to 3 tablespoons **butter** or margarine in a wide frying pan over medium-high heat. Add fish, without crowding, and cook until browned lightly on one side. Turn with a wide spatula and cook second side until lightly browned and fish flakes when prodded with a fork in thickest portion near bone.

Transfer fish to serving dish, sprinkle lightly with **salt**, and keep warm. (If you are cooking more trout, add more **butter** to pan, if needed, to about equal the quantity you started with).

Pour **butter** into a glass measuring cup. Add enough butter or margarine to make 1 tablespoon for each serving. Return butter, with an equal amount of **lemon juice**, to frying pan and heat until sizzling and very lightly browned. If desired, add ½ tablespoon of chopped **parsley** for *each* serving. Pour over fish and serve at once.

Trout with almonds

(Truite amandine)

Butter-toasted almonds contrast crisply and flavorfully with delicate trout.

For each serving allow 2 to 4 tablespoons **sliced almonds** and 1 tablespoon **butter** or margarine. In a wide frying pan, melt butter; add almonds and cook over medium heat, stirring, until nuts are toasted golden. Pour nuts and butter from pan and set aside.

Cook fish as directed for **trout with butter sauce** (recipe precedes) but don't measure and add butter. Instead, stir almonds with cooking butter into pan; stir until heated. Add ½ tablespoon *each* **lemon juice** and **parsley** for *each* serving and spoon at once over fish.

"The right pan makes the job easier."

Poached salmon

(Saumon poché)

Poaching in a flavorful liquid and serving hot or cold is an elegant way to treat salmon. You can cook a whole salmon, fillets, or steaks by poaching; each size unit requires different handling and specific directions.

The same techniques can be used to poach other fish of the same size and shape as specified for the salmon.

The French enjoy salmon simply served, perhaps with only lemon (acceptable for the more calorie conscious) or melted butter; but as you might expect, more often they enjoy it with a rich, delicate sauce. For hot fish, the sauce choice might be hollandaise (page 69), béarnaise (page 70), or mousseline sauce (page 70).

For cold salmon, the sauce might be freshly made mayonnaise (page 69), watercress mayonnaise (page 69), or a mayonnaise you flavor to taste with mustard, horseradish, green peppercorns, or capers.

For fish that is served just slightly warm, any of the sauces just listed would be appropriate —or perhaps you'd like an assortment. Allow at least ¼ cup total sauce or sauces for each serving.

Poaching liquid is flavorful and can be used in place of water in such fish soups as bouillabaisse (page 30). Strain the liquid to store; freeze if held longer than 2 days.

Poached salmon steaks. In a 10 to 12-inch frying pan, bring to boiling 2 cups **water**; 1 cup **dry white wine**; 1 small thinly sliced **carrot**; 1 small thinly sliced **onion**; 3 or 4-inch piece **celery**, thinly sliced; ½ **lemon**, thinly sliced; 3 or 4 sprigs **parsley**; 1 **bay leaf**; 8 to 10 **whole black peppers**; 4 **whole allspice**; ½ teaspoon **salt**; and ¼ teaspoon **thyme leaves**. Cover and simmer cooking broth 10 to 15 minutes.

Push vegetables to one side and slide into pan, side by side, 4 large **salmon steaks** (*each* 1 inch thick, and about ½ to ¾ pound). Cover and simmer very gently 8 to 10 minutes or until fish flakes when gently prodded in thickest portion with a fork.

Transfer to serving dish with a large slotted spatula. Serve hot, warm, or cold (cover to chill). Accompany with one or more of the **sauces** suggested in discussion on salmon poaching (above). Makes 4 servings.

Poached salmon fillets. Prepare **cooking broth** as directed for salmon steaks (preceding). You can cook as many **fillets** as will fit, uncrowded, into frying pan; allow ½ pound per serving. Fillets may be skinned, if desired.

If fillets are cut small enough to be lifted with a large spatula, they may be placed, skin side down,

(Continued on page 27)

in broth. To facilitate removal of larger fillets, wrap individually in cheesecloth before placing in broth.

Cover and simmer until fish flakes when prodded with a fork in thickest section; start testing at 5 minutes for fillets less than 1 inch thick, 8 minutes for fillets thicker than 1 inch.

Transfer to a serving dish, supporting with large slotted spatula or cheesecloth; remove cheesecloth. Serve hot, warm, or cold (cover to chill). Accompany with one or more of the **sauces** suggested in discussion on salmon poaching (page 25).

Whole poached salmon. If you cook salmon often, a fish poacher (page 7) is a good investment as it makes maneuvering the fish much easier.

Select a **whole salmon** that weighs 6 to 8 pounds. Have head, fins, and tail removed, if desired (or if necessary to fit your cooking pan).

Place salmon on rack in fish poacher that is 20 to 24 inches long (head and tail of a larger fish may have to curve up). Add 2 cups **dry white wine** and enough **water** to just cover fish. Lift out fish and set aside.

Finely chop 2 medium-size **onions**, 2 large **carrots**, and 2 stalks **celery**. Add to liquid along with 1 sliced **lemon**, 6 to 8 sprigs **parsley**, 2 **bay leaves**, 8 to 10 **whole black peppers**, 6 to 8 **whole allspice**, 1 teaspoon **salt**, and ¾ teaspoon **thyme leaves**. Bring to a boil; reduce heat, cover, and simmer poaching liquid 30 minutes. (This much can be done ahead; chill. Reheat to continue.)

Place fish on poacher rack and set into boiling liquid on high heat. Turn heat to low when boiling resumes; cover and simmer 35 to 45 minutes or until fish is pale pink in thickest portion (near bone) and flakes when prodded with a fork.

Lift salmon on rack from broth and slip onto a serving platter; if desired, peel off and discard exposed skin.

Serve hot, warm, or cold (cover to chill). Garnish with **watercress** or parsley sprigs and **lemon** pieces or slices.

To serve, cut through fish to bone. Lift from bone with a wide serving utensil. When bone is exposed, lift off and discard. Cut bottom portion of fish into serving pieces. Accompany with one or more of the **sauces** suggested in discussion on poaching salmon (page 25). Makes 12 to 18 servings.

Oven-poached whole salmon. Next to having a fish poacher, this is the most convenient way to cook a whole fish.

WHOLE POACHED SALMON is magnificent main course with new potatoes, peeled asparagus, sauces of watercress mayonnaise, hollandaise, béarnaise. Cut down to bone, lift off portions. Peel off bone and serve lower fillet.

Select a **whole salmon** weighing 6 to 8 pounds. Have head, fins, and tail removed, if desired (or if necessary to fit pan or oven). Wrap fish in cheesecloth and place flat in a large baking pan that is deeper than fish; set aside.

Prepare **poaching liquid** as directed for whole poached salmon (preceding), combining wine, vegetables, and seasonings with 4 cups **hot water**. Pour hot liquid into baking pan and add enough additional **boiling water** to cover fish.

Bake, uncovered, in a 350° oven 35 to 45 minutes or until fish flakes when prodded in thickest portion with a fork and salmon turns pale pink near bone.

Supporting fish with cheesecloth, lift from liquid and drain briefly; then place on serving platter. Remove cheesecloth.

While fish is still warm, pull off and discard exposed skin. Garnish and serve as directed for whole poached salmon (preceding). Serve hot, warm, or cold (cover to chill). Accompany with one or more of the **sauces** suggested in discussion on poaching salmon (page 25). Makes 12 to 18 servings.

Salmon in brioche

(Saumon en brioche)

French chefs have always been quick to spot a good idea; an old Russian dish called "koulibiac" (coulibiac, koulibiak—as you like) is fish sealed in a pastry and baked. The French took the concept, used buttery brioche, wrapped it around salmon, and made the dish their own.

This is a most impressive-looking and festive entrée and much easier to engineer than you might suppose. The fish is cooked ahead; the dough is started a day ahead; the grain filling is cooked ahead. At the last, you assemble these ingredients ready for baking; you can even let it rest for an hour or so before cooking, if more convenient.

Serve salmon in brioche with a simple vegetable, such as a garnish of tomatoes, cooked green beans, or asparagus.

> **Brioche dough (page 84)**
> 2 **pounds skinned salmon fillets, poached and chilled (page 25)**
> **Bulgur wheat filling (recipe follows)**
> 2 **tablespoons lemon juice**
> 3 **hard-cooked eggs, shelled and sliced**
> 1 **egg yolk beaten with 1 tablespoon water**
> **About 1 cup sour cream or ½ cup melted butter or margarine**
> **Lemon wedges**

Shape brioche dough (that has risen once at room temperature, then once in refrigerator) into smooth ball, forcing out air bubbles; pinch off about

½-cup-size portion and set aside. Flatten large ball slightly; then roll out on floured pastry cloth or muslin towel to make 12 by 18-inch rectangle.

Lay well-drained salmon fillets down center of the 18-inch length of brioche, cutting fish as necessary to form an even rectangle slightly over 4 inches wide; leave about 1-inch borders on each end. Lay sliced eggs atop fish.

With your hands, make a compact layer of bulgur wheat filling on fish. Sprinkle with lemon juice.

With pastry cloth to guide, lift sides of dough up and over filling to enclose. Pinch edges to seal securely; pull ends up so seal is on top.

Place a buttered baking sheet upside down on filled brioche. Supporting pan and pastry tautly with pastry cloth, flip brioche over onto baking sheet. Roll reserved dough out to about ¼-inch-thickness and cut in decorative shapes (leaves or flowers, or strips to use plain or to braid) and place attractively on brioche.

Lightly cover and let stand in a warm place about 30 minutes. (Or refrigerate pastry 1 to 2 hours.)

Pierce top every 2 or 3 inches, using a fork; or slash decoratively (this is *important*—otherwise steam will cause brioche to split open). Brush all over with egg yolk and water mixture.

Bake in a 350° oven 40 to 50 minutes or until dough is richly browned. Slip onto serving board or tray; cut into pieces and serve hot. Offer lemon wedges along with sour cream and/or melted butter to be added to taste. Makes 8 servings.

Bulgur wheat filling. Finely chop 1 medium-size **onion** and cook in 2 tablespoons **butter** or margarine until soft, stirring. Add ¾ cup **bulgur wheat** and cook, stirring, until lightly toasted. Add 2 cups **regular-strength chicken broth** or rich meat broth (page 16), 2 teaspoons **dill weed**, and 2 tablespoons minced **parsley**; bring to a boil, cover, and cook about 15 minutes over low heat until liquid is absorbed. Season to taste with **salt** and **pepper**. Chill before using.

Scallops in shells
(Coquilles Saint-Jacques au gratin)

In French, coquilles Saint-Jacques is the name of the scallop; to us it usually means scallops in a creamy sauce baked and served in the shell or a small casserole. Scallop shells for baking are sold in gourmet cookware shops (see page 7).

In a wide frying pan, bring ¾ cup **dry white wine** to a boil. Add 1½ pounds **scallops**, rinsed, drained, and cut into ¾-inch chunks; cover and cook on medium-low heat 3 to 4 minutes or until scallops

"little touches give the French look."

are opaque throughout (cut a gash to test).

Lift scallops from pan with a slotted spoon and set aside. Measure liquid; if more than 1 cup, boil to reduce to this amount; if less than 1 cup, add **water** to make this amount; set aside.

In same frying pan, melt 3 tablespoons **butter** or margarine. Add ¾ pound sliced **mushrooms** and cook, uncovered, on high heat, stirring occasionally, until mushrooms are limp and all liquid is evaporated. Stir in 2 tablespoons **all-purpose flour** and remove pan from heat. Slowly, smoothly, stir in reserve cooking liquid. Bring to a boil over high heat, stirring until thickened. Reduce heat to medium and stir in 1 cup shredded **Swiss cheese**, blending until melted.

Return scallops to sauce; add **salt** to taste. Spoon mixture equally into 4 scallop shells or shallow individual casseroles (about 1-cup size). Sprinkle an additional ¼ cup shredded **Swiss cheese** evenly over scallops.

Using a pastry bag fitted with a decorative tip, force 1 cup **seasoned mashed potatoes** (recipe follows) onto each shell around scallops (or into casserole around scallops)—or simply spoon potatoes in small puffs around scallops. (At this point you can cover and chill until next day.)

Bake, uncovered, in a 400° oven 15 to 20 minutes or until sauce bubbles and potatoes brown. Makes 4 servings.

Seasoned mashed potatoes. Cook and mash enough **potatoes** to make 1 cup, or prepare, according to package directions and without seasoning, enough instant mashed potatoes to make 1 cup. Add to potatoes 2 tablespoons **butter** or margarine, 1 beaten **egg**, and **salt** to taste. Use hot or cold.

Scallops provençal

(Coquilles Saint-Jacques à la provençale)

Scallops, thinly sliced, cook quickly in olive oil. Then their milky juices are reduced to a caramel-like residue that's blended with a shout of garlic to make the lightly clinging sauce.

Rinse 1 to 1½ pounds **scallops**, thinly slice, then drain. Set a wide frying pan over medium heat and add scallops and 3 tablespoons **olive oil**. Cook, uncovered, turning with a wide spatula, for about 3 to 5 minutes or until scallops become opaque.

Lift scallops from pan with a slotted spoon and set aside, leaving all juices in pan. (If done ahead, remove pan from heat.)

Turn heat to high and boil juices, stirring to keep from burning, until they become caramel in color (juices will spatter). Also drain back into pan any accumulated juices from scallops.

Stir into pan 3 or 4 tablespoons minced or pressed **garlic**, ¼ cup minced **parsley**, and scallops; stir over medium-high heat until mixture is hot. **Salt** to taste and serve at once; accompany with **lemon wedges**. Makes 3 to 4 servings.

Shrimp bordelaise

(Crevettes à la bordelaise)

When you peel the shrimp, leave on the last segment of the shell and the tail if you want the shellfish to look the way it is presented in French restaurants. Accompany with pilaf (page 68).

Peel 1½ pounds medium or large **shrimp**; leave on last segment of shell and tail, if desired. Devein shrimp.

In a wide frying pan, melt 3 tablespoons **butter** or margarine. Add 3 minced or pressed cloves **garlic**, 1½ tablespoons **lemon juice**, and ½ cup **dry white wine**. Bring to a vigorous boil, add shrimp, and cook, uncovered, on medium-high heat for 5 minutes or until shrimp turn bright pink. With a slotted spoon, lift shrimp from pan to serving dish and keep hot.

Boil juices on high heat until reduced to about ½ cup. Add 2 to 3 tablespoons minced **parsley** and pour sauce over shrimp. Makes 4 to 6 servings.

Lobster flamberge

(Homard flamberge)

Showmanship is happily unavoidable in the making of this dish; you can assemble the ingredients quickly, then cook at the table for a special supper after the theater—or even a good French film.

There is a practical side, too; a little lobster goes a long way when partnered with eggs. For a table-top preparation you will need a wide frying pan and a denatured alcohol burner (or a gas or electric fueled portable unit); a basket with the eggs; a bowl containing the measure of vermouth, sour cream, and salt; the lobster meat, detached, sliced, and returned to the shell along with the shrimp; and a dish of almonds.

In a wide frying pan over medium to medium-low heat, melt 3 tablespoons **butter** or margarine. As it melts, break 6 **eggs** into a bowl containing 2 tablespoons **sour cream** (or crème fraîche, page 77), 3 tablespoons **dry vermouth**, and ½ teaspoon **salt**. With a fork, beat until whites and yolks are blended. Pour into butter; push egg mixture from pan bottom as it cooks so liquid egg can flow down.

When eggs are still fairly liquid, add about 1 cup sliced **cooked lobster meat** (from 1 medium-size tail) and ¼ cup small **cooked shrimp**.

When eggs are set, break 2 more **eggs** into pan and stir just until cooked eggs are moistened and glazed. Sprinkle with 1 or 2 tablespoons **sliced almonds** and serve. Makes 4 servings.

Clams bordelaise

(Palourdes à la bordelaise)

Some cooks merely add hot rice to steamed clams and their liqueur. But the following method for clams bordelaise directs you to cook the rice in the same seasoned broth used for the clams; the flavors mingle much more effectively. The name "bordelaise" indicates the dish originated in Bordeaux; note the similarity of seasonings used with shrimp bordelaise (left).

Basically a light dish, though satisfying as an entrée, it can be converted to follow the current French trend of slimming foods by reducing the butter to only 1 tablespoon.

Melt ¼ cup **butter** or margarine in a 3 to 4-quart kettle. Add 1 medium-size **onion**, finely chopped; ⅓ cup finely chopped **parsley**; and 2 cloves **garlic**, minced or pressed; cook, stirring, over medium heat until onion is soft.

Add 1 can (about 14 oz.) or 2 cups **regular-strength chicken broth** (or reserved salmon poaching liquid, page 25), 1 cup **dry white wine**, and ½ cup **rice** (may be long or short grain). Bring to a boil; reduce heat, cover, and simmer 15 minutes.

Add 3 to 4 dozen well-scrubbed **clams** (suitable for steaming). Cover and simmer 5 to 10 minutes or until clams pop open. Ladle into wide soup bowls. Makes 4 servings.

Bouillabaisse

(Bouillabaisse)

The heritage of this robust soup is Mediterranean, where local fishes give it special flavor. But following the same procedure using fishes more widely available also produces delicious results.

Part of the charm of the soup is the way it is presented. The fish is lifted from the cooking kettle, and the cooking broth (which can be made ahead) is laced with cheese and served into bowls —or into cups for sipping; the hot fish is accompanied with boiled potatoes to be eaten with knife and fork. Both the broth and the fish are enlivened by a rambunctious chile and garlic mayonnaise (it, too, can be made ahead). Crusty bread and butter, green salad, and a dry white wine make for a fine repast.

    ½ cup olive oil
    1 large onion, chopped
    3 to 4 leeks, chopped (white part only)
    ½ cup lightly packed chopped parsley
    4 cloves garlic, minced or pressed
    ½ teaspoon thyme leaves
    ¼ teaspoon rubbed sage
    1/16 teaspoon ground saffron
    1 orange
    1 can (about 1 lb.) pear-shaped or
        regular whole tomatoes
    3 pounds fish trimmings (heads, tails,
        fins, bones)
    Salt
    8 cups water
    8 to 10 whole black peppers
    4 to 5 pounds assorted fish
        (suggestions follow)
    2 cups shredded Swiss cheese
    About 3 pounds hot, boiled new
        potatoes
    Hot sauce (recipe follows)

In a 5 to 6-quart kettle, combine olive oil, onion, leeks, parsley, and garlic. Cook, stirring, on medium heat until onion is soft and golden. Add thyme, sage, and saffron.

With a vegetable peeler, pare a 4-inch strip of orange peel (reserve orange for other purposes) and add to pan along with tomatoes (cut in chunks), fish trimmings, 1 teaspoon salt, and water. Cover and bring to a boil; simmer for 50 minutes. Pour broth through a wire strainer and save. Discard fish scraps and spoon vegetables back into broth. (At this point, broth can be covered and refrigerated until next day.)

Heat broth in kettle to simmering. Add peppers and fish; set fish steaks that are ¾ to 1 inch thick into broth first; return broth to simmer and cook, covered, 3 minutes. Atop steaks, place ½-inch or thinner fish steaks or fillets, small whole fish, and shellfish. Cover and quickly bring to boiling; then reduce heat and simmer gently 5 minutes more or until fish flakes when prodded with a fork in thickest portion. Remove kettle from heat at once.

Carefully lift fish from broth with slotted spoons or wide spatulas and arrange on a large platter; keep warm.

Quickly bring broth to boiling, take from heat, and, stirring constantly, sprinkle in Swiss cheese. Salt to taste and ladle into mugs or bowls.

Place hot potatoes on platter with fish. Serve hot sauce to ladle into soup and onto fish and potatoes. Makes 8 to 10 servings.

Assorted Fish. Use a combination of the following **fish steaks** (cut 1 inch thick) or fillets and shelled and deveined **shrimp**: salmon, halibut, petrale sole, Greenland turbot, turbot, rockfish, lingcod, sturgeon, whole trimmed rex sole, whole trout, whole sand dabs.

Hot sauce. In a blender or food processor, combine 1 **egg**, 3 tablespoons **wine vinegar**, 2 small **dried hot chiles**, 2 cloves **garlic**, ½ teaspoon **salt**, and 1 tablespoon **fine dry bread crumbs**. Whirl until well blended; scrape down container sides.

With machine at high speed, gradually add 1 cup **olive oil**; when thick, turn motor off and on to blend in any remaining oil. Cover and chill until ready to use; for best flavor let stand several hours. Makes about 1½ cups.

Honfleur fish stew

(Matelote d'Honfleur)

The picturesque north seacoast town of Honfleur boasts a profusion of freshly caught fish; one local offering is this stew. Choose any of the suggested boneless, white-fleshed fish to make this dish, which is lightly flavored with fennel seed and bay leaf.

Melt 2 tablespoons **butter** or margarine in a 3 to 4-quart pan over medium-high heat. Add 1 **onion**, chopped, and cook, stirring, until soft. Add 2 cans (about 14 oz. *each*) or 4 cups **regular-strength chicken broth**, 1 cup **dry white wine**, 2 medium-size **baking potatoes**, peeled and cut into 1-inch chunks, 1 **bay leaf**, and ½ teaspoon **fennel seed**. Bring to a boil; reduce heat, cover, and simmer for about 20 minutes or until potatoes are tender.

Cut in chunks 1 pound **boneless, skinned sole**, halibut, or rockfish; add to stew, cover, and simmer about 5 minutes or until fish flakes easily when prodded with a fork. **Salt** and **pepper** to taste. Ladle into serving dishes. Makes 4 or 5 servings.

BOUILLABAISSE is two-course fish soup from Provence. You start with flavorful broth in which selection of fish has cooked, then follow with fish and boiled potatoes. A hotly seasoned mayonnaise is served with broth, fish, and potatoes.

Birds and small game

"The ways of my grandmother's day are gone — but her recipes suit the family still."

Chicken, duckling, and rabbit share these pages —with a brief nod to squab and quail—for they have in common size and cooking methods. Many of the same seasonings complement one creature as well as the other, but the results differ totally.

Of a respectably lean and light nature are braised preparations of chicken or rabbit in white wine or red wine, duck or chicken with a tomato and green olive sauce, and chicken with shallots. A bit more extravagant are braised or baked dishes touched smoothly by cream and flavored by tarragon, port, or mustard.

When you're dealing with whole chicken, duckling, or squab, roasting is the cooking technique. Sometimes you stuff the bird; other times, as with the cheese-crusted chicken dish featured on the cover, you do not.

Naturally, there is an elegant orange sauce for roast duckling—its absence in a book on French cookery would be a frustration; but there is also roast duckling with an intriguing, zestful green peppercorn sauce that is delicious, light foil for the rich meat.

Dishes with chicken breasts have classical styling, with grapes, shrimp, or fillings of butter or melting cheese contributing their special character.

Set aside for the adventurous is confit de canard or salt-preserved duck (in our case, duckling). Basically, it's a simple corning process that gives the meat a quality that fascinates some, stops others in their tracks. Confit is principle in making the cassoulet, but for those who hold back on such authenticity, the cassoulet can be made instead with roast duckling.

Cheese crusted chicken with cream

(Poulet gratiné au fromage)

Roast chicken with a special, but simple, finish is shown on the cover of this book. You bake a whole chicken, then quarter it, sprinkle the pieces with cheese, and broil it briefly to develop an appetizing crust. The delicate sauce is made with the pan juices plus cream, mustard, and more cheese.

Place a 3 to 4-pound **broiler-fryer chicken**, untrussed and lightly **salted**, on a rack in a roasting pan.

Pull any fat from body cavity and lay on chicken breast (if there is no fat in chicken, brush once with melted **butter** or margarine). If desired, cook neck, gizzard, and heart on rack; place liver inside chicken.

Bake chicken, uncovered, in a 375° oven for about 1 hour or until well browned and leg moves easily when jiggled.

Cut chicken in quarters with poultry or kitchen shears. Lay pieces, skin side up, slightly apart in a shallow, heat-resistant serving dish or pan. Sprinkle chicken with ¾ cup shredded **Gruyère cheese** or Swiss cheese. Return to oven and turn off heat.

Skim and discard fat from chicken juices in roasting pan. To juices add 1 tablespoon **Dijon mustard** and ¾ cup **whipping cream** or crème fraîche (page 77); bring to a boil on high heat and stir until shiny bubbles form (takes about 3 or 4 minutes). Remove from heat and stir in ½ cup shredded **Gruyère cheese** or Swiss cheese (thin sauce, if necessary, with a little additional cream); keep warm.

Broil chicken 4 or 5 inches from heat for about 1 minute or until cheese bubbles. Pour sauce around (not over) chicken. Garnish with **watercress** and sautéed **mushrooms**, if you like. Makes 4 servings.

Brittany-style onion-stuffed chicken

(Poularde farcie aux oignons à la bretonne)

The grander scale of a roasting chicken, as compared to a broiler-fryer, is festive-looking for company meals. Tiny, slender boiled carrots are pleasing companions for the sautéed onion stuffing.

In a wide frying pan on medium heat, melt 2 tablespoons **butter** or margarine. Add 1½ pounds small whole **onions** (about 1-inch diameter) and ⅔ cup **water**. Cover and cook on medium-low heat about 15 minutes, stirring occasionally, until liquid evaporates. Turn heat to low and cook, uncovered, about 10 minutes longer, shaking pan frequently, until onions are lightly browned. **Salt** and **pepper** to taste.

Remove giblets from a 5 to 6-pound **roasting chicken** and reserve for other uses. Strip off and discard lumps of fat.

Rinse chicken, pat dry, and sprinkle lightly with **salt** inside and out. Fill body cavity with cooked onions; fasten skin shut with a skewer.

Set chicken, breast up, on a rack in a roasting pan and place neck skin under body; fold wing tips under back. Rub chicken with about 1 tablespoon room-temperature **butter** or margarine.

Bake in a 325° oven for about 2 hours or until a leg moves easily when jiggled. Transfer chicken to a platter. If you like, spoon out onions and use to garnish chicken. Spoon roasting juices into a small dish. Carve chicken and serve with juices. Makes 5 to 6 servings.

Roast chicken with sorrel stuffing

(Poulet rôti farci à l'oseille)

Here's another place for tangy sorrel, the green you can grow (page 69) which the French love to use. Fresh spinach can be substituted, but its flavor is much milder.

Remove giblets and strip lumps of fat from a 3 to 4-pound **broiler-fryer chicken**; finely chop liver and set aside. Reserve remaining giblets for other uses. Rinse chicken, pat dry, and set aside.

Melt 3 tablespoons **butter** or margarine in a wide frying pan on medium heat. Add chopped liver and cook, stirring, about 2 minutes; lift out and set aside.

To the pan add 2 tablespoons minced **shallots** or green onions and ¼ pound sliced **mushrooms**. Cook, stirring, for about 5 minutes or until mushrooms are limp and lightly browned. Stir in ¼ cup **fine dry bread crumbs**, ¼ cup **whipping cream**, 1 teaspoon **Dijon mustard**, ½ teaspoon *each* **salt** and **basil leaves**, and ¼ teaspoon *each* **pepper**, **rubbed sage**, and **thyme leaves**. Blend well and remove from heat; at once stir in 2 tablespoons minced **parsley** and 2 cups finely chopped **sorrel**.

Fill body cavity of chicken with stuffing and fasten skin shut with a skewer. Put chicken on a rack in a roasting pan; tuck neck skin under back and fold wing tips under back.

Place in a 375° oven; baste once after 20 minutes with about 1 tablespoon melted **butter** or margarine. Bake for about 1 hour or until a leg moves easily when wiggled.

Transfer chicken to a serving platter. Garnish with **parsley** and a vegetable, such as small boiled **potatoes**.

Spoon out stuffing and cut chicken in quarters with poultry shears or kitchen scissors; or carve. Accompany chicken and stuffing with roasting juices served from a small bowl to ladle onto individual portions. Makes 4 servings.

Chicken breasts veronique

(Suprêmes de volaille veronique)

"For a menu you must balance the sauces."

The name "veronique" usually indicates grapes are part of a dish, as in this handsome presentation of chicken breasts. Briefly heated, the grapes develop a jewel-like sparkle. Sautéed mushroom caps make an appropriate elegant garnish (flute caps before cooking as directed on page 58, if you like).

Bone and skin 4 large whole **chicken breasts**, *each* about 1 pound (directions follow). Cut each breast in half. Sprinkle meat lightly with **salt**.

Melt 2 tablespoons **butter** or margarine in a wide frying pan over medium heat. Add breasts and cook about 10 minutes or until lightly browned on each side.

Stir into pan 1½ tablespoons **orange marmalade**, ½ teaspoon **tarragon leaves**, and ½ cup **dry white wine**. Bring to a boil; then reduce heat, cover, and gently simmer for about 15 minutes or until chicken is white in thickest part; cut a small gash to test. (This much can be done ahead. Cover and chill; then reheat gently to continue.)

Transfer breasts to a serving dish and keep hot. Add to pan juices ½ cup **whipping cream** and bring to a rolling boil on high heat. Blend smoothly 2 teaspoons *each* **cornstarch** and **water** and stir into boiling sauce; return to a boil, stirring. Add 1½ cups **seedless green grapes** to sauce and quickly return to boiling. Pour at once over chicken. Makes 4 to 6 servings.

How to bone chicken breasts. You can bone whole or half chicken breasts in this fashion: Start at a thin (or rib) side of breast and pull or cut (using a short-bladed, sharp knife) meat from bone. Once you get going, you can slip your finger in pocket thus formed and help ease meat free up to breast bone (or keel). You will need to use knife more as you free meat near wing socket position.

If breast section is a half, cut meat free at breast bone.

If breast is whole, free meat to breast bone on either side; then grasp bone in one hand, meat in other, and pull apart.

Trim out any bits of cartilage that stick to meat. Pull off skin; save skin and bone for making rich meat broth (page 16).

Chicken breast with shrimp sauce

(Suprêmes de volaille sauce nantua)

A delicate blending of flavors—chicken breasts with pink shrimp in the sauce—has classic standing. Sautéed shrimp shells impart the nantua-style color and taste to the liquid that is then used to make the lightly clinging sauce. Pilaf (page 68) is a fine accompaniment.

Bone and skin (see left) 4 large whole **chicken breasts**, *each* about 1 pound, and sprinkle lightly with **salt**. Melt ¼ cup **butter** or margarine in a wide frying pan over medium heat. Cook chicken breasts 10 minutes, turning to brown lightly and evenly.

Warm 1 tablespoon **brandy** or cognac and set aflame; pour at once over chicken and shake pan until flame dies (*do not have beneath an exhaust fan or flammable items*).

Add 1 cup **regular-strength chicken broth** or rich meat broth (page 16). Bring to a boil. Cover and simmer about 10 minutes until chicken is white in thickest part; cut a small gash to test. (This much can be done ahead. Cover and chill; then reheat to continue.)

Lift chicken from broth and place in a serving dish; keep warm.

Add **liquid from cooked shrimp** (directions follow) and ½ cup **whipping cream** to chicken juices. Boil rapidly, uncovered, until reduced to 1½ cups. Blend smoothly 2 teaspoons cornstarch and 2 teaspoons water; stir into boiling sauce; return to a boil, stirring. Gently stir in cooked shrimp and heat through. Pour over chicken. Garnish with **lemon wedges** and **parsley** or watercress. Makes 6 to 8 servings.

Cooked shrimp. In a small pan, combine ¾ cup *each* **water** and **dry white wine**, 1 **lemon** slice, 3 or 4 **onion** slices. Simmer, uncovered, about 5 minutes. Add 1 pound medium-size **shrimp** (30 to 40 per lb.). Bring to boiling; then simmer, uncovered, for about 5 minutes or until shrimp turn bright pink; stir once or twice. Let cool in broth.

Drain off and reserve broth. Discard onion and lemon. Shell and devein shrimp, reserving shells and meat separately. Slice shrimp in half lengthwise and set aside (cover and chill if cooked ahead).

In same small pan, melt 2 tablespoons **butter** or margarine on medium-low heat; add shrimp shells and cook, mashing with a heavy spoon, for about 5 minutes. Warm 2 tablespoons **brandy**, set aflame, and pour over shells; shake until flame dies *(do not have beneath exhaust fan or flammable items)*. Add reserved shrimp broth to pan and boil rapidly, uncovered, until reduced to half (about ¾ cup). Drain off and reserve liquid (cover and chill, if made ahead); discard shells.

Chicken kiev
(Côtelette kiev)

The fascination of finding a pool of liquid butter in the center of a golden lump of chicken accounts for part of the popularity of chicken kiev; the agreeable taste explains the balance.

It's a party dish, but one you can complete ahead, except for cooking—and even when cooked, the dish can wait a few minutes before being served.

Warn guests that chicken kiev may spurt if cut into abruptly. Peeled hot asparagus (page 64) can share the seasoned butter.

This method of shaping kiev is less complex than that favored by French chefs. They like to leave a bit of wing bone on the breast and fashion mock chicken legs.

Bone and skin (page 34) 4 large whole **chicken breasts**, *each* about 1 pound.

Cut breasts in half lengthwise. Spread chicken pieces about 6 inches apart between plastic film; tuck any scraps of meat under big pieces. Firmly pound chicken with flat-surfaced mallet (do not hit hard enough to break meat apart) until each portion is no more than ⅛ inch thick. (At this point you can fold meat up in plastic film, enclose in a plastic bag, and chill until next day.)

Place a log-shaped 1-tablespoon-size lump of **butter** or margarine across narrow end of each chicken breast; you will need ½ cup (¼ lb.) in all.

Sprinkle evenly over chicken pieces a total of ¾ to 1 teaspoon crumbled **tarragon leaves**, 1 teaspoon minced or pressed **garlic**, and ½ teaspoon **salt**. Then roll up chicken from butter end. At about midpoint, fold sides in far enough to overlap and seal in butter. Continue rolling until a neat bundle is formed. With your finger tips, smooth junctions to help seal chicken to itself; fill in any holes with bits of chicken.

Coat chicken with **all-purpose flour**; then shake off excess—this also helps seal in filling. (At this point you may place pieces slightly apart in a single layer, cover, and chill until next day.)

In a 12-inch frying pan, melt 3 tablespoons **butter** or margarine (or use salad oil) over medium

heat. Add chicken and cook 15 minutes, turning frequently to brown all sides (do not pierce); if there are signs of scorching, reduce heat slightly. (If made ahead, you can set pan of chicken in a very low oven—about 150°—for as long as 30 minutes.)

Transfer chicken to a serving dish. Garnish with **lemon wedges** and **watercress** or parsley. Makes 4 to 6 servings.

Chicken cordon bleu
(Poulet cordon bleu)

Cheese, instead of butter, is the melted heart of this dish. Precede chicken with a light soup—such as potage Saint-Germain (page 17)—and serve with braised leeks (page 66) or peas with lettuce (page 66).

Follow directions for chicken kiev (preceding), but instead of filling with butter and seasoning with tarragon and garlic, place on narrow end of each breast half a 3-inch square of thinly sliced **prosciutto** or cooked ham. Place on **prosciutto** a 1-tablespoon-size rectangle of **cheese**, such as Swiss, Gruyère, jack, or cream. Sprinkle lightly, if you like, with **thyme leaves** (about ½ teaspoon, total).

Roll chicken to enclose filling. Coat with **all-purpose flour** and cook as directed. (For a crisper finish, after you coat chicken with flour, dip into 1 beaten **egg**. Then roll in **fine dry bread crumbs**—takes about ½ cup.) Makes 4 to 6 servings.

Chicken with Riesling
(Coq au Riesling ou coq au vin blanc)

Basically braised chicken, this dish takes its French character from the salt pork and white wine.

Dice ¼ pound **salt pork**. Place in a small pan and cover generously with **water**. Bring to a boil, reduce heat, and simmer, uncovered, for about 10 minutes; drain and reserve pork.

Cut 2 **broiler-fryer chickens**, *each* about 3 pounds, in serving pieces and sprinkle lightly with **salt** and **pepper**. Coat chicken pieces with **all-purpose flour**, then shake off excess.

In a wide frying pan (or 4 to 5-qt. kettle) over medium-high heat, melt 1 tablespoon **butter** or margarine with 1 tablespoon **salad oil**. Add chicken and brown pieces well on all sides without crowding. As pieces are browned, remove from pan to make room for more. Set chicken aside.

Add reserved salt pork to frying pan along with 3 medium-size **carrots**, cut in 1-inch lengths, and 12 small whole **onions** (about 1-inch diameter). Cook, stirring, until onions are lightly browned. Return chicken to pan along with ¼ cup chopped **shallots** or green onion.

Warm ¼ cup **cognac** or brandy and set aflame; at once pour over chicken (*do not have beneath an exhaust fan or flammable items*). Shake pan until flame dies.

Stir in 1½ cups **Riesling-type dry white wine** (such as Johannisberg Riesling), ¾ pound small **mushrooms** (quartered, if large), and 2 tablespoons minced **parsley**. Cover and simmer about 30 minutes or until thigh is tender when pierced. **Salt** and **pepper** to taste. Makes 6 to 8 servings.

Rabbit in wine with mushrooms

(Lapin aux champignons et au vin blanc)

The similarity in the ways you can prepare chicken and rabbit is tastefully demonstrated here. Carrots vichy (page 64) are good with the rabbit.

Cut 1 **fryer rabbit**, about 2½ pounds, in serving-size pieces and sprinkle lightly with **salt**. Place a wide frying pan over medium-low heat; add ¼ cup **olive oil** and the rabbit; brown pieces well on all sides. Lift rabbit from pan and set aside.

Add to pan ¾ pound small **mushrooms** (or large mushrooms, quartered); cook on medium heat, stirring, until lightly browned and all juices have evaporated. Remove pan from heat, stir in 2 tablespoons **all-purpose flour**, and blend in 1½ cups **dry white wine**, 8 to 10 small whole **onions** (about 1½-inch diameter), ¼ cup chopped **parsley**, ¼ teaspoon **rosemary leaves**, and 2 cloves **garlic**, minced or pressed. Cover; simmer 45 minutes or until meat is tender when pierced.

Meanwhile, melt ¼ cup **butter** or margarine in a frying pan. Add 2 cups **garlic-flavored croutons** and stir until well coated with butter and lightly toasted.

Place rabbit in a shallow serving dish and surround with toasted croutons. Sprinkle with chopped **parsley** or garnish with a sprig of rosemary. Makes 4 servings.

Rabbit in mustard sauce

(Lapin à la moutarde)

The mildness of rabbit takes well to the nippy seasonings of this golden sauce. The sauce is generous enough to be deliciously shared with a simple vegetable, such as small boiled potatoes or braised leeks (page 66).

Cut 2 **fryer rabbits**, *each* about 2½ pounds, in serving pieces. Sprinkle lightly with **salt**; then coat with **all-purpose flour**, shaking off excess.

Melt 5 to 6 tablespoons **butter** or margarine in a wide frying pan and brown rabbit, without crowding, on medium heat. Cook pieces in sequence, setting browned pieces aside. Return all rabbit and any juice to pan. Warm ¼ cup **brandy**, set aflame, and at once pour over rabbit, shaking pan until flame dies (*do not have beneath an exhaust fan or flammable items*). Lift rabbit from pan and place in a deep 3½ to 4-quart casserole.

In frying pan cook 1 pound small **mushrooms** (quartered, if large), and ½ cup minced **shallots** or green onion, and ¼ cup minced **parsley** in 3 more tablespoons **butter** until shallots are soft but not browned. Blend in 2 tablespoons **Dijon mustard**, 2 cups **whipping cream**, and 2 tablespoons **lemon juice**; bring to a boil; then pour over rabbit in casserole. (This much can be done ahead; cover and chill.)

Cover rabbit and bake in a 375° oven for about 50 minutes (about 1 hour, if chilled) or until rabbit is tender when pierced.

Drain or siphon juices from casserole and place in a wide frying pan. Bring juices to a full, rolling boil. Beat 3 **egg yolks** to blend, add some of the hot liquid, then stir yolk mixture into frying pan and at once reduce heat to low. Cook, stirring constantly, until sauce thickens; do not boil. Pour sauce over rabbit and sprinkle with chopped **parsley**. Makes 8 servings.

Stuffed roast squab on toast

(Pigeonneaux farcis sur canapés)

Roasted squab on toast is a handsome way to present these dark-fleshed, distinctively flavored birds.

You may have to order squabs from the market well ahead of the day you plan to serve them, and you may have to make several calls before you locate them. If the birds are frozen, thaw completely.

Rinse 4 **squabs**, *each* about 1 pound, and pat dry. Reserve livers; use remaining giblets for other purposes such as rich meat broth (page 16). Fill body cavities evenly with **mushroom and liver stuffing** (directions follow) and skewer skin to hold shut.

Place birds, slightly apart, on a rack in a roasting pan, with wing tips folded under back. Drape

ELEGANTLY PRESENTED in garden is rabbit in mustard sauce with braised leeks. Rabbit bakes gently with an abundance of mushrooms in cream made bold by generous dollop of distinctive Dijon mustard.

a **bacon** slice back and forth over each breast (4 slices total).

Bake in a 375° oven 50 minutes to 1 hour or until birds are well browned, basting with pan juices several times during cooking. After 30 minutes, push bacon from breasts into pan so breasts will brown.

Trim crusts from 4 slices **firm white bread**. Melt ¼ cup **butter** or margarine in a wide frying pan over medium heat; add bread and cook, turning, until golden brown; set aside. About 3 minutes before serving, place toast on a flat pan in oven with squab.

To serve, place toast on a serving platter. Lift squabs from pan and set one on each piece of toast; accompany with bacon. Skim fat from juices; spoon juices into a bowl to pass. Makes 4 servings.

Mushroom and liver stuffing. Melt ¼ cup **butter** or margarine in wide frying pan. Add ¼ pound chopped **mushrooms**, 4 **chicken livers**, the **squab livers** (if available), ¼ cup chopped **shallots** or green onion. Cook, stirring occasionally, on medium heat until livers are firm but still slightly pink in centers (cut a gash to test). Let stand until cool enough to touch; then chop and mix with ½ cup finely chopped **cooked ham** and ½ cup coarsely chopped **pistachios** (salted or unsalted). Season mixture to taste with **salt** and **pepper**.

Chicken sauté with shallots

(Poulet bonne femme)

"Bonne femme" is the "good wife," and when her name is attached to a dish it indicates simplicity, good taste, and practical ingredients. Chances are the choices of the bonne femme for her family cooking may become your own as well.

Cut a 3 to 4-pound **broiler-fryer chicken** in serving pieces and sprinkle with **salt**. Melt ¼ cup **butter** or margarine in a wide frying pan on medium heat. Add chicken and brown pieces well on all sides (takes about 20 minutes).

Push chicken to one side of pan and place in empty area ¼ cup finely chopped **shallots** or green onion, 1 tablespoon minced **parsley**, ½ teaspoon **tarragon leaves**, and 1 teaspoon **chervil leaves** (optional). Cook and stir until shallots are soft. Gently shake pan to mix seasonings among chicken pieces.

Pour in 1 cup **dry white wine**. Cover and simmer gently for about 30 minutes or until chicken thigh or leg is tender when pierced. (At this point you can cover and chill dish; reheat to continue.)

Transfer chicken to a warm serving dish; if desired, skim most fat from pan juices and pour juices over chicken. Garnish with **parsley** or watercress sprigs. Makes 4 servings.

Chicken marengo

(Poulet marengo)

Truffles and crayfish, plus eggs and chicken—from these the original chicken marengo was fashioned. A premium on truffles and, in some areas, a scarcity of crayfish resulted in the version that follows. The fried egg garnish and the tomato sauce mingle harmoniously with the chicken.

With so many flavors, the dish shows off well as a separate course. Start with soup, such as potage de légumes (page 19), and follow with green salad and cheese (page 71).

Cut a 3 to 4-pound **broiler-fryer chicken** into serving pieces and sprinkle with **salt** and **pepper**.

Pour 3 tablespoons **olive oil** or salad oil into a wide frying pan on medium heat. Add chicken and brown evenly on all sides (takes about 20 minutes). Transfer chicken to a shallow casserole (about 2-qt. size).

To frying pan add 2 medium-size peeled, seeded, and chopped **tomatoes** (or ¼ cup tomato paste), 1 clove minced or pressed **garlic**, ½ pound small **mushrooms** (quarter, if large), and ½ cup **dry white wine**. Bring to a rolling boil, stirring, and cook 2 or 3 minutes. Taste for **salt**, adding if needed. Pour sauce over chicken. (This much can be done ahead; cover and chill.)

Cover chicken and bake in a 350° oven for 40 minutes (50 minutes if chilled) or until a leg or thigh pierces easily; cook uncovered during last 20 minutes of baking.

Meanwhile, cut a heart shape or round from *each* of 4 to 6 slices **firm white bread**, using most of each slice. Melt 6 tablespoons **butter** or margarine in a wide frying pan and add bread. Cook on medium to medium-low heat, turning as needed, until toasted a golden brown. Set aside.

Just before chicken is ready to serve, set fried toast in a flat pan in oven with chicken to warm

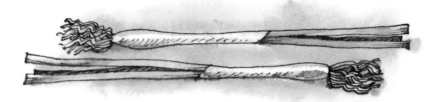

for 2 or 3 minutes. In frying pan, fry 4 to 6 **eggs** (add **butter** if needed) until as set as you like; then, using a biscuit cutter, cut each into a neat round with yolk in center.

Lift chicken from juices and place on a platter; skim and discard fat from sauce. Pour sauce over chicken and sprinkle with 1 or 2 tablespoons minced **parsley**. Place toast pieces around chicken and set a fried egg on each piece. Makes 4 to 6 servings.

Chicken with port cream
(Poulet au porto)

Port, cream, and the chicken juices thickened with egg yolks make a shiny glaze for the pieces of meat.

Cut a 3 to 4-pound **broiler-fryer chicken** in serving pieces and sprinkle lightly with **salt**.

Melt 3 tablespoons **butter** or margarine in a wide frying pan over medium heat. Add chicken and brown on all sides (takes about 20 minutes). Pour into pan ½ cup **port** and ¾ cup **whipping cream**. Cover and simmer gently for about 30 minutes or until thigh is tender when pierced. (At this point you can cover and chill chicken; reheat to continue.)

Lift chicken from pan and place in a serving dish. Boil juices on highest heat until reduced to about 1⅓ cups. Beat 2 **egg yolks** and blend some of the hot liquid into them; then stir yolk mixture into sauce in pan. Cook over low heat, stirring constantly, until sauce thickens slightly. *Do not boil.* Pour sauce over chicken and garnish with 1 or 2 tablespoons chopped **parsley**.

Accompany with hot **fried shoestring potatoes** (prepare one 12-oz. package frozen shoestring potatoes according to package instructions). Makes 4 servings.

Chicken with green olives
(Poulet aux olives)

Two kinds of olives—mellow, green ripe ones and tangy Spanish-style—balance each other in this robust dish. Serve with pilaf (page 68) or cooked Swiss chard.

Cut a 3 to 4-pound **broiler-fryer chicken** in serving pieces. Place a wide frying pan over medium heat, add ¼ cup **olive oil** or salad oil and chicken pieces. Brown well on all sides (takes about 20 minutes). Lift chicken from pan and set aside.

To pan add 1 medium-size **onion**, finely chopped, and 2 large cloves **garlic**, minced or pressed. Cook, stirring, until onion is soft.

Add ½ cup **tomato sauce**, 1¼ cups **water** or rich meat broth (page 16), 1 can (6 oz.) drained **pitted green ripe olives**, and 1 jar (3 oz.) drained **Spanish-**

style pitted olives (with or without pimento stuffing). Stir sauce, return chicken to pan, cover, and simmer for about 30 minutes or until thigh is tender when pierced. **Salt** to taste. Makes 4 or 5 servings.

Duckling with green olives
(Canard aux olives)

If you've had only roasted duck, you'll find this a good way to get to know how succulent the meat can be when braised. This dish is popular in the Bistro Allard on the Parisian left bank. The seasonings are the same as for chicken with green olives, but the results are very different.

Cut a 5 to 6-pound **duckling** in serving pieces and sprinkle lightly with **salt**; discard chunks of fat.

Place in a wide frying pan over medium-low heat (to control spattering); cook, uncovered, until well browned, turning pieces as needed (include giblets, if desired), for about 45 minutes. Lift duck from pan and set aside. Pour all but ¼ cup of fat from pan.

To pan add 1 medium-size **onion**, finely chopped, and 2 large cloves **garlic**, minced or pressed. Cook, stirring, until onion is soft. Add ½ cup **tomato sauce**, 2½ cups **water** or rich meat broth (page 16), 1 can (6 oz.) drained **pitted green ripe olives**, and 1 jar (3 oz.) drained **Spanish-style pitted olives** (with or without pimentos). Stir sauce, return duck to pan, cover, and simmer on low heat until tender when pierced (about 1 hour). **Salt** to taste and skim off fat. Makes 4 or 5 servings.

Chicken with tarragon cream
(Poulet à la crème d'estragon)

Slowly brown the chicken; then make the sauce with the pan juices. Serve with green peas or cauliflower.

Cut a 3 to 4-pound **broiler-fryer chicken** in serving pieces and sprinkle lightly with **salt**. Melt ½ cup (¼ lb.) **butter** or margarine in a wide frying pan. Add chicken and cook, uncovered, on low to medium-low heat for about 45 minutes or until browned well on all sides and thigh is tender when pierced. Transfer chicken to a serving platter and keep hot.

(Continued on next page)

Add to pan ¾ pound small **mushrooms** (quartered, if large) and cook, uncovered, on medium-high heat until lightly browned and all liquid is evaporated; stir often.

Blend ½ teaspoon **tarragon leaves** and ⅓ cup **whipping cream** with mushrooms. Bring to boiling. Mix a little of hot liquid with 2 slightly beaten **egg yolks**; then stir yolk mixture into pan. Reduce heat to very low and stir constantly until sauce thickens slightly. *Do not boil.* Pour sauce over chicken. Makes 4 servings.

MATTHEW NAYTHONS

ON MARKET DAY in French country village, freshness of hen destined for kitchen cannot be challenged.

Chicken with Beaujolais

(Coq au Beaujolais ou coq au vin)

If you use a varietal wine, then you name the dish by the wine, such as chicken with Beaujolais or Zinfandel or Chateau Smith-Lafitte. Sometimes the chicken is marinated in the wine, sometimes not.

Trim bone from 1 **pork shoulder steak** (about ⅓ lb.) and cut meat in ½-inch cubes. In a wide frying pan (or 4 to 5-qt. kettle) cook pork in its own fat over medium-high heat, stirring, until meat is very well browned and crisp; set aside.

Cut a 3 to 4-pound **broiler-fryer chicken** in serving pieces. Add chicken and 8 small **onions** (about 1 to 1½-inch diameter) to pork fat. Cook, uncovered, over medium heat for about 20 minutes or until chicken and onions are well browned on all sides. Lift meat and vegetables from pan and set aside.

To same pan add ½ pound small **mushrooms** (quartered, if large) and cook, stirring occasionally, until lightly browned and all juices have evaporated. Lift mushrooms from pan and add to chicken.

Pour 1 can (14 oz.) or 2 cups **regular-strength beef broth** or rich meat broth (page 16) into frying pan and boil on high heat, uncovered, until reduced to 1 cup.

Return chicken, onions, and mushrooms to pan. Stir in 1 cup **Beaujolais** (or any dry red wine) and 2 tablespoons **Dijon mustard**; bring to boil, reduce heat, cover, and simmer on low heat for about 30 minutes or until thigh is tender when pierced. Stir in reserved pork and 2 tablespoons chopped **parsley**.

When simmering again, lift meats and vegetables from pan with a slotted spoon and transfer to a serving dish. Blend 1 teaspoon **water** smoothly with 1 teaspoon **cornstarch** and stir into cooking juices; bring to a boil, stirring; then pour over chicken. Makes 4 servings.

Roast duckling with green peppercorn sauce

(Canard au poivre vert)

Crisp, rich duckling and piquant, lean sauce flavored by green peppercorns produce a delicious play of taste and texture contrasts.

Place a 5 to 6-pound untrussed **duckling** (thawed, if frozen) on a rack in a roasting pan. Strip off and discard chunks of fat. Fold neck skin under duckling. Reserve liver for other uses; if desired, place remaining giblets and neck on rack alongside duck.

Pierce skin of duckling every few inches with a fork; then sprinkle lightly with **salt**.

Place in a 325° oven and bake for 3 to 3½ hours or until leg moves easily when jiggled.

Meanwhile, finely chop 1 small **red onion** and place in a small frying pan with 4 tablespoons **red wine vinegar**, ½ teaspoon **tarragon leaves**, and ¼ teaspoon **thyme leaves**. Boil, uncovered, stirring until all liquid is evaporated.

Measure 2 to 3 tablespoons **canned green peppercorns** into a wire strainer; rinse under cool running water and drain. Add to onions the peppercorns, 1 teaspoon **basil leaves**, 2 teaspoons **Dijon mustard**, and 1½ cups **regular-strength beef broth** or rich meat broth (page 16). Boil, uncovered, until reduced to about 1¼ cups; set aside.

(Continued on page 42)

BRIGHT SCATTERING of parsley is final seasoning for chicken cooked in red wine. You start by browning bits of pork, then chicken, onions, and mushrooms. Dry red wine of your choice, blended with broth, makes tasty sauce.

Protecting your hands, lift duckling and drain juices from body cavity into roasting pan. Transfer duckling (and giblets and neck, if desired) to a serving platter and keep hot.

Spoon or siphon as much fat as possible from pan drippings (there will be an abundance of fat); discard fat. Stir drippings to loosen all browned particles (add about ¼ cup **water**, if needed) and pour into green peppercorn sauce. Boil rapidly, stirring occasionally, until again reduced to about 1¼ cups. Add 2 tablespoons minced **parsley** and pour into a serving dish.

Cut duck into quarters with poultry shears or kitchen scissors. Pass sauce to spoon onto individual plates. Makes 4 servings.

Roast duckling with orange sauce

(Canard à l'orange)

The specialty of French restaurants the world around is duck with a mildly sweet orange sauce. If there is any secret, it is to present the sauce alongside the meat, for the skin instantly loses its delicious crispness when moistened.

Wild rice (or a blend of white and wild rice) takes well to the orange sauce, too.

With a vegetable peeler, pare thin orange-colored skin from 3 medium-size **oranges**. Cut skin into 1/16-inch-wide strips that are about 1 inch long; reserve oranges. Bring 3 cups **water** to boiling, add peel, reduce heat, and simmer, uncovered, for 15 minutes. Drain, reserving peel.

Roast a 5 to 6-pound **duckling** as directed for roast duckling with green peppercorn sauce (preceding; omit sauce), placing ⅓ of the orange peel in duck body cavity; reserve giblets.

Place giblets (including liver, if desired) in a small pan with 1 medium-size finely chopped **onion**, 1 finely chopped **carrot**, 1 **bay leaf**, and 3 cups **regular-strength chicken broth** or rich meat broth (page 16). Bring to a boil, reduce heat, cover, and simmer about 1½ hours or until giblets are very tender; **salt** to taste. Pour off and reserve liquid; finely chop and reserve giblets. Discard bay leaf and vegetables. Boil liquid rapidly, uncovered, until reduced to 2 cups.

In another small pan, boil ¼ cup **wine vinegar** with 3 tablespoons **sugar** until mixture begins to caramelize and turn golden brown. At once add giblet liquid. Set aside until duckling is cooked.

Protecting your hands, lift duckling and drain juices from body cavity into roasting pan. Transfer bird to a serving platter and keep hot.

Spoon or siphon off all fat possible from drippings; discard fat.

Add ½ cup **port** or madeira to drippings and stir to free all browned bits. Pour drippings into giblet broth, add reserved orange peel, and bring to boiling. Blend 2 tablespoons **cornstarch** with 3 tablespoons **water**, stir into boiling sauce, and cook, stirring, until boiling resumes. Add 1 tablespoon **cointreau** or other orange-flavored liqueur; **salt** to taste. Pour into a serving bowl and keep warm.

Peel white membrane from reserved oranges and slice oranges crosswise. Garnish duck with fruit; cut duck into quarters with poultry shears or kitchen scissors. Pass sauce to spoon onto individual plates. Makes 4 servings.

"Orange is a good perfume for duck."

Quail with vine sauce

(Cailles à la sauce vignoble)

On each of these tiny birds there are only a few bites; the meat is firm and takes on seasonings readily.

Quails must be ordered from the market (allow some time to find them) unless the hunter can provide the table with either quails or pigeons.

Tie the wings and legs to the bodies of 4 to 6 dressed **quails** or band-tail pigeons (6 to 12 oz. *each*). Coat birds with **all-purpose flour**; then shake off excess.

Melt ¼ cup **butter** or margarine in a wide frying pan and brown birds on all sides over medium-low heat; take care not to let butter scorch.

Measure ¾ cup **regular-strength beef broth** or rich meat broth (page 16) and add ½ of it to frying pan along with ¼ cup **port**, 2 or 3 tablespoons **raisins**, and 2 **whole cloves**. Cover and simmer for 30 minutes, adding balance of broth as needed to keep liquid level about constant.

You will need 6 **canned grape leaves**, or 6 fresh grape leaves that have been immersed in boiling water for about 1 minute (snip off stems).

To serve, place a bird on a grape leaf and spoon sauce equally over all. Allow 1 bird for each person as a first course, 2 for each as a light entrée.

Confit: salt preserved duck

Rocamadour is a hillside village in the Dordogne region of France, famed for the production of foie gras and dishes made of duck livers—hence the abundance of duck and geese to salt for confit.

Confit de canard—salt-preserved duck (or duckling)—is not everyone's dish. Redolent of garlic, both raw and braised, confit must be classified as earthy peasant food. But those who enjoy the rich flavor of duck that has a tang similar to that of corned beef will find confit intriguing.

Going one step further, salted duck (or goose) is a traditional flavoring element for cassoulet, the great bean casserole (see right). You have an option, though, when it comes to making cassoulet —instead of salted duckling you can use regular roast duckling for a quicker version.

Salted duck, Rocamadour-style

(Confit de canard à la Rocamadour)

Cut a 5 to 6-pound **duckling** in serving pieces; cut breast in half lengthwise. You can salt neck, gizzard, and heart, but reserve duck liver for other purposes; discard chunks of fat.

Measure ¼ cup **salt** and use all to rub over every surface of duckling. Pack pieces in a bowl (glass, ceramic, or stainless steel). Cover and refrigerate for 24 to 48 hours (the longer it stands, the saltier the flavor).

Rinse each piece of duckling well under cool running water, pat dry.

In a wide frying pan (or 4 to 5-qt. kettle) arrange duck pieces side by side. Cook, covered, over medium-low heat in its own fat for about 1½ hours or until thigh is very easy to pierce—turn duck as needed to equalize cooking—it doesn't become brown and crisp, but surfaces do take on a pale brown color.

Lift duck pieces from drippings and drain briefly on absorbent material; then place on a serving platter and keep hot. Pour off all but about 2 tablespoons duck fat. Reserve fat to use for cassoulet or for sautéing other meats or vegetables, if you like—though some find its saltiness objectionable; store, covered, in refrigerator.

To cooking pan, add 5 to 6 cloves minced or pressed **garlic** and cook, stirring, over medium heat until soft. Add ½ cup **water** and bring to a boil, stirring to scrape free all browned bits. Blend in ¼ cup chopped **parsley**; when wilted, pour sauce over duckling.

Accompany with hot **fried shoestring potatoes** (prepare one 12-oz. package frozen shoestring potatoes according to label directions) sprinkled with 2 tablespoons minced **parsley** and 1 clove minced or pressed **garlic**. Makes 4 servings.

Bean casserole with salted duck

(Cassoulet au confit de canard)

Salt a **duckling** according to directions at left, but refrigerate for only 24 hours.

Because confit de canard is salty, it is necessary to control the saltiness of the ham shanks used to flavor the cassoulet.

Combine 2 pounds **smoked ham shanks** with 4 quarts **water** in a 4 to 5-quart kettle. Bring to a boil, reduce heat, and simmer, uncovered, 5 minutes. Drain and repeat this step; taste water and if even slightly salty, drain and simmer one more time; drain again.

Sort through 1 pound **dried small white beans**, picking out any foreign material. Rinse beans and place in a 4 to 5-quart kettle with ham shanks. Add 6 cups **water**, 5 to 6 sprigs **parsley**, 1 **bay leaf**, 1 teaspoon **thyme leaves**. Bring to a boil, reduce heat, cover, and simmer gently for about 2 hours; stir occasionally. Lift out shanks and discard skin, fat, and bone. Return meat to beans.

Meanwhile, cook **salted duck**, **Rocamadour-style** (at left) through browning step—but *do not add garlic and parsley; also do not prepare potatoes.* Reserve cooking fat and set duckling pieces aside. (Cover and chill if made ahead.)

Finely chop 2 medium-size **onions** and cook until soft in ¼ cup of the **confit fat**.

When beans have cooked 2 hours, add onions and fat to them along with ½ cup **tomato paste**. (At this point you can cover and chill beans until next day; reheat to continue.)

Pour bean mixture into a wide 4 to 5-quart casserole (or use cooking kettle if it can go into oven). Cover and bake in a 325° oven for 2 hours or until beans are creamy textured to bite; add a little more water if beans seem dry—they vary in the amount of water they absorb.

Tuck into casserole 1 pound thickly sliced **garlic sausages**, lay confit onto surface of beans, and bake, uncovered, 30 minutes more to heat through.

In a small frying pan on medium heat, melt 6 tablespoons **confit fat**, add 1 cup **croutons**, and cook, stirring, until golden. Stir in 3 cloves minced or pressed **garlic** and ¼ cup minced **parsley**. Sprinkle onto cassoulet. Serves 8 to 10.

Cassoulet without confit. Cook **beans** as directed (preceding); use **butter**, margarine, or roast duckling fat in which to cook **onion** and **croutons**. Meanwhile, roast a 5 to 6-pound **duckling** as directed for roast duckling with green peppercorn sauce (page 40); omit sauce. (You can use same oven in which beans are baking.)

When duck is done and beans are cooked, cut duck in serving pieces. Skim fat and discard; stir drippings into beans. Arrange duck on beans; garnish with croutons. Serves 8 to 10.

Hearty meats

"A good cook is a practical cook."

One of the great culinary skills to learn from the French is how to handle meat. Skilled as they are at showing off the quality of premium cuts, they are equally adept at turning the least costly cuts into magnificent dishes.

Stewing meats and often overlooked accessory meats become memorable when carefully cooked and judiciously seasoned. Consider lamb stew as a party-scale navarin; veal stew as a succulent and delicate blanquette; or even slivers of tripe slowly, slowly baked to melting tenderness in the fashion favored by Normandy.

The more costly roasts of the leg or loin of pork, lamb, or veal are often used interchangeably with the modestly priced shoulder of these animals when the meat is lightly seasoned, roasted, and complemented principally by the meat juices. At other times, the roast may be simmered, such as to make veal with tuna sauce.

For really grand occasions, the fillet of beef becomes an entrée for two as chateaubriand or as the very showy, make-ahead boeuf en croute (beef in crust, boeuf Dürnstein, or beef Wellington, as you prefer).

Ground beef—as hamburgers à la Française—provides imaginative contrast, and for elegance with speed, sautéed steaks (of varying price categories) are seasoned in a number of ways.

Here you will find also such classics as choucroute garnie, veal Orloff, paupiettes, jambon persillé à la bourguignonne, pot au feu, all worked out in easy-to-manage steps.

Keep in mind that each dish in this chapter has the styling and quality suitable for guests.

Madame Morier's roast pork

(Rôti de porc Madame Morier)

Good-flavored juices that evolve as the meat roasts become the light and well-seasoned sauce. Cooked vegetables, such as slender carrots, make an attractive addition to the serving platter.

Place a 2½-pound **boned**, **rolled**, **and tied pork loin roast** (shoulder end, center, or loin end) in a small, shallow roasting pan. Rub onto meat ½ teaspoon **thyme leaves** and ¼ teaspoon **rubbed sage**; then lightly sprinkle with **salt**. Finely chop 1 medium-size **onion** and place around meat. Add ¼ cup **regular-strength chicken broth** or rich meat broth (page 16).

Bake, uncovered, in a 325° oven for about 2 hours or until a thermometer inserted in thickest part of meat registers 180°.

After 1 hour pour an additional 1¼ cups **regular-strength chicken broth** or rich meat broth into pan; stir to free any browned particles. Baste meat once or twice with juices.

When meat is done, remove from oven; heat ¼ cup **madeira** and set aflame (*not under an exhaust fan or flammable items*), pouring at once over roast. Lift meat onto a serving platter and keep warm.

Set roasting pan on high heat and stir as juices come to boiling. Blend until smooth 1 tablespoon **cornstarch** and 1 tablespoon **water**. Stir mixture, a little at a time, into juices until sauce is consistency you like. Pour sauce into a bowl. Pass to spoon onto sliced roast. Makes 6 or 7 servings.

Roast pork with prunes

(Rôti de porc aux pruneaux)

Prunes, plumped in the roasting meat juices, are a popular companion for pork in several regions in France.

Follow directions for **Madame Morier's roast pork** (preceding), omitting herbs and onions. As you add the 1¼ cups liquid to pan, also add 12 to 16 **pitted dried prunes**. When you remove roast from juices, also lift out prunes and arrange around roast. Thicken juices as directed and pass to spoon onto sliced meat and fruit. Makes 6 or 7 servings.

Pork with red cabbage

(Porc au choux rouges)

The meat nestles in a bed of cabbage and apples as it cooks in the oven. For this dish from the Lorraine region, hot buttered noodles are a typical companion.

Mix together ¾ teaspoon **thyme leaves**, ½ teaspoon **salt**, ¼ teaspoon *each* **pepper** and **ground allspice**, and 1 clove **garlic**, minced or pressed. Rub mixture evenly onto surface of a 2½ to 3-pound **boned, rolled, and tied pork loin roast** (shoulder end, center, or loin end). Cover meat and chill at least 2 hours or until next day.

Melt ¼ cup **butter** or margarine in a wide frying pan or 5 to 6-quart kettle. Add 1 small **onion**, thinly sliced; 1 medium-size **carrot**, chopped; and 2 cloves **garlic**, minced or pressed; cook on medium heat, stirring occasionally, for 5 to 10 minutes or until vegetables are soft but not browned.

With a sharp knife, finely shred 1 medium-size (about 2 lb.) **red cabbage**; add cabbage to cooked vegetables along with 2 cored and chopped **tart apples**, 2 tablespoons **vinegar**, and ⅛ teaspoon **ground nutmeg**. Cook, stirring, on medium-high heat until cabbage is limp. Spoon vegetables into a large, shallow casserole (4 to 6-qt. size).

In cooking pan on medium heat, melt 1 tablespoon **butter** or margarine with 1 tablespoon **salad oil**. Add seasoned pork roast and brown well on all sides. Make a well in center of cabbage large enough to hold roast, and place meat in dish. Insert a meat thermometer in thickest part of roast.

In pan, bring to boil 1 cup **dry red wine** with 1 **bay leaf**; pour over cabbage. Cover casserole. Bake in a 325° oven for about 2 hours or until thermometer registers 180°.

If you want to serve from cooking container, drain off juices and save. (Or transfer meat to a platter and lift vegetables onto platter with a slotted spoon.) Keep meat warm while you rapidly boil juices down to about 1 cup.

Cut meat in about ½-inch-thick slices; pass sauce to spoon individually onto meat and cabbage. Makes 6 to 8 servings.

Sauerkraut with all the trimmings

(Choucroute garnie)

Have a crock of Dijon mustard, sour pickles, and potatoes boiled in their skins (or "dressing gowns," as the French say) to go with this festive and hearty Alsatian specialty. Juniper berries give a faint woodsy flavor to the sauerkraut.

Empty 2 large cans (about 1 lb. 13 oz. *each*) **sauerkraut** into a colander; rinse thoroughly under cold running water. Drain well.

Put sauerkraut in a shallow 4-quart casserole. Mix in 2 peeled, cored, and thinly sliced **apples**, ⅛ pound diced **salt pork** *or* 4 slices bacon, 6 **whole black peppers**, 6 **whole juniper berries**, and 1 cup **dry white wine**.

Cover and bake in a 300° oven for 4 hours,

adding **meats** at intervals—choose a total of 3 to 4 pounds from the following:

After 2 hours tuck in with sauerkraut 1 whole (about 1 lb.) **coteghino sausage** *or* a 1-pound piece French-style white wine sausage (salsicce vin blanc).

After 2½ hours lay on sauerkraut 1 to 2 pounds **smoked pork chops** (*each* cut about ½ inch thick) or a 1 to 2-pound slice cooked ham.

After 3½ hours tuck into sauerkraut 4 **Polish sausages** (about 1 lb.), *or* 4 or 5 (about ¾ lb.) German veal frankfurters or old-fashioned frankfurters, *or* about ¾ pound tiny cocktail-size frankfurters. If you like, cut larger sausages in thick slices, chops or ham into serving-size portions; arrange on sauerkraut before serving. Makes 8 to 10 servings.

Parsleyed ham, Burgundy-style

(Jambon persillé à la bourguignonne)

Thin slices of ham are rippled through the parsley-flecked aspic in this handsome cold entrée. Sometimes chunks or thick slices of ham are used instead, but the meat is less effectively flavored by the aspic. Garnish with cucumber slices, tomatoes, and more parsley. The dish makes a good first course, too.

Mix 2 envelopes **unflavored gelatin** with ½ cup **cold water** and let stand a few minutes to soften; set aside. Bring to boiling over high heat 2 cans (about 14 oz. *each*) or 3½ cups **regular-strength chicken broth** or rich meat broth (page 16), 2 tablespoons **white wine vinegar**, and ¼ teaspoon **liquid hot pepper seasoning**. Add softened gelatin, stirring until dissolved; remove from heat.

Chill gelatin until slightly thickened. Gently stir in ½ cup *each* thinly sliced **green onion** and lightly packed minced **parsley**; pour mixture into a 6-cup ring mold. Using a spoon, lightly push individual pieces of very thinly sliced **cooked ham** (you'll need about ¾ lb. total) down into gelatin to create a rippled effect. Cover mold and chill until set (at least 6 hours) or until next day.

To unmold, dip container up to rim in hottest tap water just until edges liquefy. Cover container with serving plate and invert ham aspic onto plate; chill briefly to firm surface.

Accompany with **mustard sauce** (recipe follows). If you like, garnish with **hard-cooked egg** slices or parsley. Cut salad in thick slices with a sharp knife. Makes about 6 servings.

Mustard sauce. Mix well together 1 cup **mayonnaise**, ½ cup **crème fraîche** (page 77) or sour cream, 3 tablespoons **Dijon mustard**, and 2 teaspoons **sugar**.

Madame Morier's roast veal

(Rôti de veau Madame Morier)

The same seasoning Madame Morier used for pork on page 45, she uses for veal as well. Creamed spinach (page 68) or creamed sorrel (page 68) are the vegetables she likes with this veal.

The juices can be poured through a wire strainer for a smooth-looking sauce, but you may feel the onions are really too tasty to discard.

Place a 3½ to 4-pound **boned, rolled, and tied veal shoulder** or leg roast in a small, shallow roasting pan. Rub onto meat ½ teaspoon **thyme leaves** and ¼ teaspoon **rubbed sage**; sprinkle lightly with **salt**. Finely chop 1 medium-size **onion** and place around meat. Add ¼ cup **regular-strength chicken broth** or rich meat broth (page 16).

Bake, uncovered, in a 325° oven for about 2 hours or until a thermometer inserted in thickest part of meat registers 170°. After 1 hour pour an additional 1¼ cups **regular-strength chicken broth** or rich meat broth into pan, stirring to free any browned particles; baste meat once or twice with juices.

When meat is done, remove from oven; heat ¼ cup **madeira** and set aflame (*not under an exhaust fan or flammable items*), pouring at once over roast. Lift meat onto a serving platter and keep warm.

Set roasting pan on high heat and stir as juices come to boiling. Blend until smooth 1 tablespoon **cornstarch** and 1 tablespoon **water**. Stir mixture, a little at a time, into juices until sauce is consistency you like. Pour sauce into a bowl. Pass to spoon onto sliced roast. Makes 7 or 8 servings.

Veal roast Orloff

(Rôti de veau Orloff)

A complex-looking, make-ahead party dish, this veal roast is stuffed when partially cooked. You slice meat and insert the seasonings—onion sauce, ham, and cheese—then retie the roast and complete the cooking later.

The roast you buy must be rolled and tied; roasts held in place by a net casing will not work.

Sprinkle a 3 to 4-pound **veal sirloin tip** (or boned, rolled, and tied leg or shoulder roast) lightly with **salt**. Place fat side up (if there is any fat) on a rack in a shallow roasting pan.

Bake, uncovered, in a 325° oven for about 2 hours (or 1¾ hours for leg or shoulder) until a meat thermometer inserted in thickest section registers 160°.

Remove from oven and let roast rest 15 minutes; place roast in a flat pan.

To make room for filling, cut roast in this fashion: make ½-inch-wide slices, cutting across grain and down through roast to within ½ inch of bottom; discard any loose strings. Spread 1 cut side of each slice generously with half the **soubise sauce** (recipe follows). Insert a thin slice of **cooked Canadian bacon** (you'll need ½ lb. total) on sauced side of each slice; then place alongside bacon a thin slice of **Gruyère cheese** or Swiss cheese (you'll need about 6 oz. in all).

To reshape roast, tie a string around it horizontally to bring slices snugly together.

With cut side up, return roast to rack in shallow pan. Spread remaining soubise sauce on top of roast and sprinkle top with about 2 tablespoons shredded **Gruyère cheese** or Swiss cheese. (If made ahead, cover loosely and chill until next day.)

To complete cooking, place roast in 325° oven and bake about 45 minutes (55 minutes if chilled) or until meat is heated through and sauce topping is lightly browned. Cut between slices to serve. Makes 8 to 10 servings.

Soubise sauce. Cook 1 chopped small **onion** in 2 tablespoons **butter** or margarine on medium heat until onion is soft; stir frequently. Purée cooked onion with butter in a blender, food processor, or food mill.

Return onion to pan and stir in ½ cup unsifted **all-purpose flour**, ½ teaspoon **salt**, ¼ teaspoon **ground nutmeg**, and a dash of **pepper**. Cook on medium heat, stirring, for about 2 minutes.

Remove from heat and gradually, smoothly, stir in ½ cup **regular-strength chicken broth** or rich meat broth (page 16) and ½ cup **whipping cream**. Bring to a boil, stirring constantly. Blend a little hot sauce into 1 beaten **egg yolk**; then stir yolk mixture into pan and remove from heat. Use hot; or cover, chill, and use cold.

Veal with tuna sauce

(Veau à la sauce au thon)

Better known by its Italian name, "vitello tonnato," cold veal roast with tuna sauce is also classic with the French, who tend to have a more delicate hand with the sauce.

Lay 6 canned **anchovy fillets** on inside surface of a 4 to 5-pound piece of **boned veal leg** or shoulder; then roll roast and tie securely every 1½ to 2 inches. Also make one horizontal tie to keep roast secure.

Place meat in a 5 to 6-quart kettle. Add 1 large **onion**, chopped; 2 medium-size **carrots**, sliced; 1 stalk **celery**, sliced; 4 cloves **garlic**; 6 sprigs **parsley**; 2 teaspoons **thyme leaves**; 1 **bay leaf**; and ½ teaspoon **salt**. Add equal amounts of **dry white wine** and **water** to almost cover roast (takes about 3 cups *each*).

Insert a meat thermometer in thickest part of roast, positioning so it is not in liquid and so you can cover pan. Set lid in place.

Bring liquid to a boil, reduce heat, and simmer gently for about 1½ hours or until thermometer registers 160°.

Remove from heat and let meat chill in broth— it should be refrigerated at least 6 hours but can be held as long as 2 days.

Lift meat from broth (reserve broth for soup, sauces, or other uses) and cut in about ¼-inch-thick slices; discard string.

Arrange slices overlapping on a serving platter. Mask evenly with **tuna sauce** (recipe follows); place any extra sauce in a bowl to be added to meat as desired when served.

Garnish veal with drained **capers**, **black ripe olives**, strips of canned **pimento**, and **parsley** or watercress. Makes 10 to 12 servings.

Tuna sauce. In a blender or food processor, whirl 1 can (6 to 7 oz.) undrained **tuna** until a paste. If desired for an ultra-smooth sauce, force paste through a fine wire strainer; discard fibrous remains; set tuna aside.

Rinse blender or food processor and add 1 **egg**, 3 tablespoons **lemon juice**, 2 teaspoons **Dijon mustard**, and 4 canned **anchovy fillets**. Whirl until smooth; then with motor running, add 1½ cups **olive oil** or salad oil (or part of each) in a steady but very slow stream at first, then a bit faster in about a ¹⁄₁₆-inch-wide stream as mixture begins to thicken. When all oil is added, turn off motor and stir in 1 tablespoon drained **capers** and tuna. Cover and chill; sauce is best if made 5 or 6 hours ahead (can be held 2 or 3 days).

Stuffed veal rolls

(Paupiettes de veau)

Slices of veal, pounded thin, are filled with garlic, herb, and bacon stuffing. The rolls are braised and a sauce is made with pan juices. Tomatoes gratin (page 68) and pilaf (page 68) or hot noodles are suitable companions.

Trim connective tissue and any fat from a 2-pound piece of **boned veal leg**. Slice meat across grain into ¼-inch-thick pieces.

Place meat between sheets of clear plastic film, allowing several inches between pieces. Pound gently but firmly with a flat-surfaced mallet until meat is about ¹⁄₁₆ inch thick.

Following natural division of meat as much as possible, cut into rectangles about 3½ by 6 inches. (At this point you can wrap meat in plastic film, slip into a plastic bag, and chill overnight.)

(Continued on next page)

Mince 1 pound **bacon** (or cut in chunks and grind in a food processor) and blend with ¼ cup minced **parsley**, ½ teaspoon *each* **tarragon leaves**, **basil leaves**, **thyme leaves**, and **rosemary leaves**, and 2 cloves **garlic**, minced or pressed.

Place about 1 tablespoon of this mixture on each pounded piece of veal and spread to within ½ inch of sides. Fold long sides up onto filling; then roll up meat from narrow end, keeping folded sides turned in. Secure rolls with short skewers or tie on each end with string. (At this point you can cover and chill rolls until next day.)

Place 3 tablespoons **butter**, margarine, or salad oil in a wide frying pan on medium heat. Add meat and brown evenly on all sides, turning as needed.

To pan add ¾ cup **dry white wine**, ¾ cup **regular-strength chicken broth** or rich meat broth (page 16), ⅓ cup *each* minced **onion** and minced **green pepper**, 2 sprigs **parsley**, 1 **bay leaf**, ¼ teaspoon **thyme leaves**, and ⅛ teaspoon **pepper**. Bring to boiling; then reduce heat, cover, and simmer very gently for about 25 minutes or until meat is tender when pierced.

Place veal on a serving platter, remove strings or skewers, and keep meat warm.

Pour cooking liquid through a wire strainer; reserve liquid and discard residue. Return liquid to frying pan. Blend 1 tablespoon **cornstarch** with 2 tablespoons **water**. Bring cooking liquid to a boil; stirring, add cornstarch paste, a little at a time, until sauce is consistency you like. Pour hot sauce over meat and serve. Makes 6 to 8 servings.

Alsatian stew
(Beckenoffe)

Rich in juices, beckenoffe is best served in wide soup bowls. Pass crusty bread, cut in chunks, and follow with a green salad. You use a fruity white wine to give the dish its Alsatian character.

Peel 4 medium-size (about 1 lb. total) **new potatoes** and cut in ¼-inch-thick slices. Make a layer of half the potatoes in a deep 3 or 4-quart casserole.

Combine 1 pound **boneless veal stew** (from shoulder or breast), cut in 1-inch chunks, with 1 pound **boneless pork stew** (from shoulder or butt), cut in 1-inch chunks. Top potatoes in casserole with half the meat.

Thinly slice 2 medium-size **onions**, chop ⅓ cup packed **parsley**, mince or press 2 cloves **garlic**, and set out 2 **bay leaves**. Put half the onion, parsley, garlic, and bay leaf on meat.

Cover with remaining potatoes, veal, pork, onion, parsley, garlic, and bay leaf. Sprinkle with 1 teaspoon **salt** and ¼ teaspoon **pepper**. Pour in 1¾ cups (1 half-bottle or ⅘ pt.) **dry white Rhine-type wine**, such as Riesling, Johannisberg Ries-

"When there are juices left from the roast or the meat, save them to flavor vegetables for another meal."

ling, Gewurztraminer, or Sylvaner. Lay a ¼-cup chunk of **butter** or margarine on top.

Cover and bake in a 375° oven for 1 hour and 30 minutes or until meats are tender when pierced. Makes 6 servings.

White stew of veal, pork, or lamb
(Blanquette de veau ou ragoût à l'ancienne)

The meat is not browned, but simmers in its own juices as the first step in making this succulent, cream-finished stew.

With veal, it becomes the classic blanquette de veau. The same technique is excellent with pork or lamb, giving you ragoût à l'ancienne.

Peas with lettuce (page 66) and little new boiled potatoes are attractive companions for any version of this stew.

Cut 2 pounds **boneless veal stew** in about 1½-inch chunks (or use boneless pork stew from butt or loin end, or lamb stew from neck or shoulder; trim excess fat from meat). Place meat in a 3 to 4-quart pan, add ¼ teaspoon **thyme leaves**, 5 or 6 **whole black peppers**, 1 clove **garlic**, 3 to 4 sprigs **parsley**, 1 **bay leaf**, and 1 medium-size **onion**, minced.

Cover and cook over medium heat, stirring occasionally, for 30 minutes (juices will cook out of meat). Then add ½ cup **dry white wine** and 1 can (about 14 oz.) or 2 cups **regular-strength chicken broth** or beef broth, or rich meat broth (page 16). Simmer gently, covered, about 1 hour longer or until meat is very tender when pierced. If desired, add 6 to 12 small whole **onions** (about 1½-inch diameter) about 30 minutes after you add liquid.

Lift meat and whole onions from juices and set aside. If desired, discard parsley and bay leaf.

To pan add 1 cup **whipping cream** or crème fraîche (page 77). Boil rapidly, uncovered, stirring until large shiny bubbles form and sauce thickens (takes 7 to 10 minutes). Return meat, onions, and any juices to sauce and heat through. (If made ahead, chill, covered; then reheat, adding a little broth if needed.) Add **salt** and **lemon juice** to taste. Makes about 6 servings.

Sweetbreads in aspic with filbert mayonnaise

(Ris de veau en aspic à la mayonnaise noisette)

Tender, pale lumps of sweetbreads, sealed in a flavorful, sparkling aspic, are deliciously sauced by crisp toasted filberts in fresh mayonnaise. Serve this unusual dish as an entrée following a sturdy soup such as potage de légumes (page 19), or as a first course before a light main dish, such as an omelet.

> Cooked sweetbreads (directions follow)
> Clarified broth (directions follow)
> Lettuce leaves
> Filbert mayonnaise (directions follow)

Combine sweetbreads with broth and pour into a 1-quart, straight-sided, deep container, such as a terrine or loaf pan. Cover and chill until firmly set (at least 6 hours or until next day).

Cut mold into slices (at least ½-inch-thick) and lift from terrine, supporting with a wide spatula. Place on lettuce leaves on serving plates. Pass filbert mayonnaise to spoon onto individual servings. Makes 4 main-dish or 6 first-course servings.

Cooked sweetbreads. In a pan (at least 3-qt. size), bring to a boil 2 quarts **water**, 2 pounds **sweetbreads**, 2 teaspoons **salt**, and 2 tablespoons **lemon juice**. Reduce heat, cover, and simmer 15 minutes. Drain and let stand until cool enough to handle. When cool, remove as much of the white connecting membranes as possible (using a sharp knife if necessary); break sweetbreads into bite-size pieces. (At this point, sweetbreads can be covered and refrigerated 1 to 2 days.)

Clarified broth. In a pan (at least 4-qt. size), bring to a boil 2 cans (14 oz. *each*) or 4 cups **regular-strength beef broth**; 1 pound **bony chicken pieces** (such as wings or backs); 1 *each* medium-size **onion, carrot**, and **turnip** (*each* cut in chunks); 5 **whole black peppers**; and 1 **bay leaf**. Reduce heat and simmer, covered, 1 hour.

Pour broth through a wire strainer or colander and discard residue. Chill broth; lift off and discard all fat. (At this point, broth can be covered and refrigerated 1 or 2 days.)

Beat 2 **egg whites** until foamy. Heat broth to boiling; then whip egg white into boiling broth. Return to a full boil, remove from heat, and let stand until slightly cooled.

Moisten a muslin cloth with cold water and wring dry; use it to line a wire strainer placed over a large container. Pour broth through cloth without flooding—egg white slows draining. Draw up cloth into a bag and gently squeeze out as much liquid as possible; discard whites. Boil liquid until reduced to 1¾ cups.

Soften 1 envelope **unflavored gelatin** in ¼ cup **cold water**. Add to simmering broth and stir until dissolved. Use hot or warm; or if made ahead, chill, covered, and reheat to liquefy.

Filbert mayonnaise. Place ½ cup **filberts** on a rimmed baking sheet. Bake, uncovered, in a 325° oven 10 to 20 minutes or until skins begin to split and nut meat is golden. Shake pan frequently to toast nuts evenly.

Remove from oven. When filberts are just cool enough to touch, rub nuts, a few at a time, briskly between your hands to loosen as much of the brown skin as possible. Blow away loose skins. Coarsely chop nuts and set aside.

In a blender or food processor, whirl until mixed 1 **egg**, 2 teaspoons **Dijon mustard**, and 1 tablespoon **wine vinegar** or lemon juice.

With motor on high speed, add 1 cup **salad oil**, a few drops at a time in the beginning; then increase flow to a slow, steady stream about 1/16 inch wide as mixture begins to thicken. When all oil is incorporated, stir in filberts. Serve; or cover and chill as long as 1 to 2 days before using.

Boiled tongue

(Langue de boeuf bouillie)

The affinity of plain boiled tongue for flavorful sauces and zesty condiments makes it a flexible dish. Serve the tongue hot or cold with mustard or horseradish, or season with one of the simple sauces that follow.

Rinse well in **cool water** a 3 to 3½-pound **beef tongue**; then place in a deep 4 to 5-quart kettle. Add 1 large **onion**, cut in chunks, 2 **bay leaves**, 6 **whole cloves**, 1 teaspoon **salt**, and enough **water** to just cover meat.

Bring to a boil, reduce heat, cover, and simmer gently for about 3 hours or until tongue is very tender when pierced.

Let tongue cool in broth; then lift out and peel off exterior skin and discard. Also cut away any small bones and fat at base of tongue. (At this point you can cover and chill tongue in broth; reheat in broth if you want to serve tongue hot.)

Slice tongue thinly across grain and serve hot or cold with **prepared mustard** or prepared horseradish. (Reserve broth to use in soup or to prepare the following tongue dishes.) Serves 6 to 8.

Tongue with gribiche sauce

(Langue de boeuf à la sauce gribiche)

An ideal make-ahead luncheon dish, the meat is good hot or cold.

Prepare **boiled tongue** according to preceding directions and serve hot or cold with this sauce.

Blend ⅔ cup **olive oil**; ⅓ cup **wine vinegar**; 2 tablespoons *each* minced **parsley**, chopped drained **capers**, and minced **sour pickles**; 2 tablespoons minced **shallot** or green onion, 3 finely chopped **hard-cooked eggs**; and ½ teaspoon **tarragon leaves**. Makes 6 to 8 servings.

Tongue provençal

(Langue de boeuf à la provençale)

Hot mashed potatoes or purée of cauliflower can share the sauce with the tongue.

Cook **boiled tongue** according to preceding directions. Slice meat (hot or cold) and set aside; reserve ½ cup **cooking broth**.

Combine in a wide frying pan 1 large **onion**, chopped; 1 large **green pepper** (or red), seeded and chopped; 1 clove **garlic**, minced or pressed; and 2 tablespoons **olive oil** or salad oil.

Cook over medium heat, stirring, until vegetables are soft. Blend in 2 cans (8 oz. *each*) **tomato sauce**, ½ teaspoon **thyme leaves**, reserved tongue broth, and sliced tongue. Cover and simmer gently for about 30 minutes to blend flavors. Serve hot. Makes 6 to 8 servings.

Liver lyonnaise

(Foie à la lyonnaise)

Liver sautéed to moist perfection is topped with a piquant onion sauce quickly made in the same cooking pan.

Trim away and discard any membranes and tubes from 1 to 1½ pounds **calf liver** or baby beef liver; cut in ½-inch-thick slices. Coat liver with **all-purpose flour**; shake off excess. **Salt** lightly.

In a wide frying pan on medium-low heat, melt 2 tablespoons **butter** or margarine and add 2 tablespoons **olive oil**. Lay liver slices side by side in pan and cook, uncovered, turning as needed to brown, for about 8 minutes or until liver has lost almost all pink color in center (cut a gash to test). Lift liver from pan to a serving dish and keep warm.

To pan add 1 large **onion**, minced, and 1 tablespoon **wine vinegar**. Boil, stirring, until liquid evaporates. Add ½ cup **dry red wine** and boil rapidly, stirring, until liquid is reduced to 3 or 4

tablespoons. Spoon onion sauce onto liver and serve. Makes 3 to 5 servings.

Drouant's veal kidneys on skewers

(Rognons de veau à la Drouant en brochette)

The secret to cooking kidneys properly is not to overdo. Broil just until firm—overcooking toughens them.

Allow 1 **veal kidney** (about 4 oz.) for each serving. Cut out fatty membrane and split kidneys lengthwise.

Thread 1 or 2 kidney halves on each metal skewer, arranging to keep kidneys secure and flat (loose ends curl when heated).

Broil on a rack 3 to 4 inches from heat for 5 to 6 minutes to a side for firm, moist kidneys; baste occasionally with melted **butter** or margarine.

Meanwhile blend 6 tablespoons room-temperature **butter** or margarine with 2 tablespoons minced **parsley** and ½ teaspoon grated **lemon peel**.

To serve, remove kidneys from skewers, **salt**, and squeeze fresh **lemon juice** over them. Accompany with lemon butter for topping, allowing about 1 tablespoon for a serving.

Tripe, Caen-style

(Tripes à la mode de Caen)

Long, slow cooking makes tripe tender and gives seasonings time to mingle. Some feel the dish is best made on one day and served the next.

Rinse well in **cool water** 3 pounds **tripe**; drain and cut in 2-inch squares.

Place tripe in a deep 8-quart casserole and add 2 pounds **veal shank** (whole or cut in chunks); 3 large **onions**, finely chopped; 4 medium-size **carrots**, finely chopped; 3 **leeks**, well washed and sliced (including some green top); 1 cup chopped **parsley**; 8 cloves **garlic**, minced or pressed; 2 teaspoons **salt**; 1½ teaspoons **thyme leaves**; and ½ teaspoon **pepper**. Mix ingredients to blend.

Chop 2 tablespoons **beef fat** or veal fat and sprinkle over contents of casserole; then pour in ½ cup **calvados** or brandy and 4 cups **apple cider**.

Place a tight-fitting lid on casserole (if lid does not fit snugly, you can make a flour paste of 6 to 8 tablespoons **water** and 1 cup **all-purpose flour** and spread in a thick layer around lid to make a seal).

Bake in a 300° oven for 10 hours; tripe must be very tender. Remove lid (you may have to crack off flour paste) and lift out veal bones; return any attached meat to casserole and discard bones. (If made ahead, tripe can be covered and chilled, then reheated.)

In a kettle, simmer, uncovered, at least 30 minutes. **Salt** to taste. Serve in wide soup plates. Makes 8 servings.

Rack of lamb with juniper sauce

(Carré d'agneau à la sauce au genièvre)

Juniper berries—usually associated with game—lend an aura of the woods and delicate wildness to domesticated meat as well.

Buy 2 **rack of lamb roasts** (*each* about 2 lb.). Have meatman remove back bone or crack between rib bones to facilitate carving.

Rub all surfaces of meat with 1 clove **garlic**, peeled and halved; reserve garlic for use in basting sauce.

Combine 1 teaspoon **salt**, ⅛ teaspoon **pepper**, and 2 teaspoons **whole juniper berries**, crushed. Sprinkle over meat; then with your hands press seasonings into all surfaces.

Place roasts fat side up, side by side, in a single layer in roasting pan. Bake, uncovered, in a 350° oven for 20 minutes. Then brush with **juniper berry basting sauce** (recipe follows).

Continue roasting, basting 3 or 4 times, for 20 to 25 minutes longer or until thermometer inserted in thickest part of one roast registers 145° to 150° for pink meat (cook to 160° for medium-well done, to 175° for well done). Place meat on platter and keep warm.

Skim and discard fat from drippings. Measure remaining basting sauce; then add enough **water** to make 2 cups.

Pour into drippings and stir to free browned particles. Bring to boiling. Blend 2 tablespoons **water** smoothly with 4 teaspoons **cornstarch**; stir into boiling sauce; return to a boil, stirring.

Serve sauce to be spooned individually onto carved portions of lamb. Makes 4 to 6 servings.

Juniper berry basting sauce. In a small pan heat together ½ cup **regular-strength beef broth** or rich meat broth (page 16) and ½ cup **dry red wine** (or use 1 cup broth); reserved **garlic**, minced or pressed; and 1 tablespoon **whole juniper berries**. Bring to a boil, reduce heat, and simmer for 10 minutes. Use hot or cold.

Stuffed lamb shoulder, provençal

(Épaule d'agneau farcie à la provençale)

Stuffed with a mixture of ground pork and olives, this boneless lamb roast is easy to carve. Because of the pork inside, the roast cooks to 170°.

Thoroughly mix ½ pound **lean ground pork**; 1 clove **garlic**, minced or pressed; ¼ cup finely chopped onion; ½ cup sliced **pimento-stuffed Spanish-style olives**; ¼ teaspoon *each* **salt** and **thyme leaves**; dash **pepper**; 1 **egg**; 3 slices **whole-wheat bread**, crusts trimmed and bread cut in ½-inch cubes; and 2 tablespoons **milk**.

Fill cavity of a 3-pound **boned lamb shoulder roast** with pork mixture; sew edges closed with string. Rub **olive oil** lightly over surface of meat.

Place stuffed roast on rack in pan, fat side up. Bake, uncovered, in a 325° oven about 2 hours and 15 minutes or until meat thermometer inserted in the thickest part registers 170°.

Place meat on a serving platter; remove strings, if desired. Keep meat warm while you make sauce.

Skim fat from roasting pan. Add to pan ¾ cup **regular-strength chicken broth** or beef broth, or rich meat broth (page 16); stir to free browned bits.

Smoothly blend 2 tablespoons **water** with 2 teaspoons **cornstarch**. Bring pan juices to boiling and stir in cornstarch, a little at a time, until sauce is consistency you like. Slice roast and spoon sauce onto meat slices. Makes 6 servings.

Leg of lamb, Port Saint Germain-style

(Gigot Port Saint-Germain)

Flageolets—mild, green-tinged, dried beans—are the Parisians' choice to go with leg of lamb. A parsley butter goes well with both.

Have a 5 to 6-pound **leg of lamb** boned, rolled, and tied. Cut 1 large clove **garlic** in slivers. Cut small gashes in surface of lamb and insert garlic slivers. Sprinkle meat lightly with **salt** and set on a rack in a roasting pan.

Bake in a 325° oven for 1½ to 2 hours or until a meat thermometer in center registers about 145° (for pink interior). Rub meat once or twice during cooking with a lump of **butter** or margarine.

Transfer lamb to a large, rimmed serving dish. Spoon on one side of meat 5 to 6 cups hot cooked and drained **flageolets** (page 65) or frozen baby lima beans (about two 10-oz. packages). On other side of roast, arrange 2 cups **watercress** sprigs or pieces of curly endive (chicory).

Slice meat and serve with vegetables. Place a dollop of **parsley butter** (recipe follows) on each serving of meat. Pass **lemon wedges** to squeeze on servings, as desired. Makes 6 to 8 servings.

Parsley butter. Thoroughly blend 2 tablespoons minced **parsley** and 1 clove minced or pressed **garlic**

with 6 tablespoons room-temperature **butter** or margarine. Chill, covered, if made ahead. Serve at room temperature.

Miche's leg of lamb

(Gigot à la Miche)

France's favorite Sunday dinner is leg of lamb with white beans (page 65). The leg, trimmed of its fat, then dotted with garlic and coated with butter, is decidedly milder in flavor than an untrimmed roast.

Trim most tough skin and surface fat from a 5 to 6-pound **leg of lamb**. Cut 3 or 4 cloves **garlic** in slivers and insert into small gashes in surface of lamb. Rub lamb with 2 to 3 tablespoons room-temperature **butter** or margarine and sprinkle lightly with **salt**. Place in a shallow pan or casserole slightly larger than roast.

Bake, uncovered, in a 325° oven for 1½ to 2 hours for meat that is still pink near bone (about 145° on meat thermometer). Lift lamb to a serving dish.

Blend 1 cup **regular-strength chicken broth** or rich meat broth (page 16) with pan drippings, stirring to free browned bits. Pour into a sauce dish and skim off fat.

To serve lamb, grasp narrow end of leg (protect hands with a small cloth) and slice meat, cutting parallel to leg bone. Serve juices with meat. Makes 6 to 8 servings.

Burgundy-style beef stew

(Boeuf bourguignon)

Wine, beef, onions, and mushrooms are the essence of this satisfying stew. You start the meat on top of the range, but it finishes cooking, untended, in the oven.

Heat 1 tablespoon **olive oil** or salad oil in a wide frying pan. Add 1½ to 2 pounds **boneless beef stew**, cut in about 2-inch chunks, and brown well over medium-high heat.

Push meat to one side of pan; sprinkle 2 teaspoons **sugar** in empty area and position this over most direct heat (medium-high). When sugar begins to caramelize, add 2 teaspoons **wine vinegar** and stir to blend in caramel and meat.

Remove from heat; lift meat from pan with slotted spoon and place in a deep 2-quart casserole.

To pan add ¾ cup *each* **dry red wine** and **regular-strength beef broth** or rich meat broth (page 16). Bring to a boil, stirring to free all browned particles. Add ¾ teaspoon **salt** and ¼ teaspoon **pepper** and pour mixture over meat.

Add 1 more tablespoon **olive oil** or salad oil to

frying pan along with 1 large **onion**, thinly sliced. Cook, stirring, on medium heat until onion rings are limp and translucent. Stir into casserole.

Cover casserole and bake in a 375° oven for 2 to 2½ hours or until meat is very tender when pierced.

Meanwhile, melt 2 tablespoons **butter** or margarine in frying pan. Add 1½ pounds sliced **mushrooms** and cook, stirring, on medium-high heat until liquid evaporates and mushrooms are lightly browned.

In a small covered pan, cook 6 small whole **onions** (about 1 to 1½-inch diameter) in **boiling water** to cover for about 20 minutes or until tender when pierced; drain.

Add onions to pan with mushrooms and gently mix, cooking, until onions are also lightly glazed. When meat is cooked, stir in mushrooms and onions and bake 10 minutes more to heat vegetables. Makes 6 servings.

Boiled beef with vegetables

(Pot au feu)

This whole-meal production originates from one kettle. Present the collection of vegetables and tender beef ribs from a platter and the cooking broth from a tureen. Then serve together into wide bowls as a knife-and-fork soup.

Arrange 4 or 5 slender, **marrow-filled beef bones** (each 3 or 4 inches long) in a large, deep kettle (at least 12-qt. size). Set on bones about 6 pounds **lean beef short ribs** cut in 3 to 4-inch lengths.

Add 3 quarts **water**, 8 to 10 sprigs **parsley**, 1 medium-size **onion** studded with 6 **whole cloves**, 4 cloves **garlic**, 1 **bay leaf**, 1 teaspoon **thyme leaves**, and 1 teaspoon **salt**. Bring to a boil, reduce heat, cover, and simmer gently for 2 to 2½ hours or until meat is quite tender when pierced.

Have ready 6 medium-size **new potatoes** (1½ to 2-inch diameter), scrubbed well; 6 small **turnips** (1½ to 2-inch diameter, or use large turnips cut in pieces); 6 medium-size **carrots**; 1 **celery root** (about 1 lb.; optional), cut in sixths; and 6 **leeks**, washed well (split tops down to solid white area and hold under running water to remove soil) and trimmed of all but a little green stem.

Add all vegetables but leeks to simmering meat, pushing them down into liquid as much as possible.

(Continued on page 55)

TO CARVE LEG OF LAMB French-style, slice meat off parallel to bone. Those who like their meat well done get outside slices; pinker lamb is from inner slices. Spoon meat juices onto servings of boiled white beans.

Navarin: party stew for 20

Grandly scaled, navarin is a handsome lamb stew and a practical party entrée with many make-ahead steps. The large quantity of meat cooks in the oven, requiring much less attention than it would if prepared over direct heat.

Springtime lamb stew

(Navarin à la printanière)

A plain navarin contains only turnips—and occasionally potatoes—with the lamb, but it becomes navarin à la printanière, or springtime lamb stew, regardless of the season, when you use a greater variety of vegetables.

Because of the many vegetables, you need only salad, bread (perhaps the large brioche, page 85), and a grand dessert such as oeufs à la neige (page 79) for a fabulous meal.

>   10 **pounds boned lamb shoulder (4 or 5 shoulder roasts)**
>   3 **tablespoons sugar**
>   ½ **cup unsifted all-purpose flour**
>   1 **tablespoon salt**
>   4 **cans (14 oz. *each*) or 8 cups regular-strength beef broth or rich meat broth (page 16)**
>   1 **teaspoon rosemary leaves, crumbled**
>   2 **bay leaves**
>   **Hot cooked vegetables (directions follow)**
>   2 **packages (10 oz. *each*) frozen petite peas, thawed**

Trim excess fat from lamb and place fat in a large baking pan (such as a broiler pan about 11 by 13 inches). Bake fat, uncovered, in a 500° oven for 10 minutes, stirring occasionally.

Meanwhile cut lamb into about 2-inch cubes or chunks. Remove pan from oven, measure and reserve 6 tablespoons fat, and discard remainder.

Put 3 tablespoons reserved fat in another baking pan of about equal size. Add half the meat to each pan and mix with fat. Spread meat out so that pieces are separated as much as possible and are in a single layer. Then sprinkle with sugar.

Bake meat in a 500° oven for 20 minutes, uncovered, to draw juices; stir several times. Alternate pan positions in oven after first 10 minutes.

Drain all juices from meat and reserve. Mix flour with salt and sprinkle evenly over meat, mixing to blend well. Return meat, uncovered, to oven and bake 20 minutes, stirring occasionally. Switch pan positions after first 10 minutes.

During this time, boil reserved pan juices until reduced to about 1 cup. Divide juices, broth, rosemary, and bay leaves evenly between 2 pans of meat, stirring to free browned particles in pans. Cover pans with close-fitting lids or foil.

Bake in a 375° oven for about 1½ hours or until meat is very tender.

Gently transfer meat pieces to a large bowl. Pour pan juices through a wire strainer and reserve; discard residue. Skim as much fat from juices as possible; then add juices to meat. (At this point you can refrigerate meat, covered, until next day.)

Unless you have an 8-quart (or larger) serving container in which you can cook, you will need to continue using 2 baking pans; divide meat and liquid evenly between them.

Cover meat and reheat in a 300° oven for at least 1 hour, stirring occasionally. Then add all the cooked vegetables (hot or cold) and heat, covered, for at least 1 hour or as long as 2 hours. One hour before serving, gently mix in peas.

To serve, baste surface of navarin with some of the juices. Makes 20 servings.

Hot cooked vegetables. You will need 20 medium-size **carrots** (or 60 very small carrots), 20 small whole **onions** (1 to 1½-inch diameter), 15 to 20 medium-size **turnips**, 20 small new **potatoes** (1 to 1½-inch diameter), and 6 to 10 very small **crookneck squash**. You can cook carrots, onions, and turnips the day before, but potatoes have better flavor, squash better texture if not reheated.

Peel medium-size carrots, dividing each into thirds and trimming blunt ends to simulate very small carrots. Peel turnips and cut any that are more than 1 inch in diameter into sections no thicker than 1 inch, trimming to make rounded shapes. Peel onions.

In covered pans, cook carrots, turnips, and onions *separately* in **boiling salted water** to cover, just until vegetables are easy to pierce (each requires about 15 minutes); drain well.

Add vegetables to meat. Or, if done ahead, follow this procedure: immerse hot vegetables in ice water. When chilled, drain and package airtight. Refrigerate until next day. Gently mix into meat, according to preceding directions.

Peel potatoes and cook, covered, in **boiling salted water** to cover for 15 to 20 minutes or until easy to pierce. Drain and add to meat according to preceding directions.

Cut stem and blossom ends from squash and cut each in half lengthwise or into ½-inch-thick slices. Cook, covered, in **boiling salted water** to cover for about 8 minutes or until easy to pierce. Drain and add to meat according to directions.

Cover and simmer 30 to 40 minutes or until vegetables are just tender. After 15 minutes, lay leeks onto meat and vegetables.

Carefully lift vegetables from broth with slotted spoon and arrange on a large platter; lift out meat and place on platter. Keep hot. If desired, shake marrow from marrow bones onto platter, also.

Pour broth through a fine wire strainer (or colander lined with cheese cloth) and save; discard bones, seasonings, and clove-studded onion.

Skim as much fat as possible from broth.

Serve broth from a tureen to ladle into wide soup bowls. Then pass platter of meat and vegetables and add a selection to each bowl. Accompany with a **hot prepared mustard** or Dijon mustard and **prepared horseradish**. Makes 6 servings.

"When you cook for a large affair, sometimes you must change the way things are done."

Beef in casserole

(Boeuf en daube)

"Daube" comes from daubière, the name of the type of covered earthenware container in which this dish was originally made. For this stew, the faint tang of orange is a characteristic seasoning.

Cut 6 slices **bacon** into 1-inch pieces and place in a wide frying pan. Cook on medium-low heat, stirring occasionally, until bacon is brown and crisp. Lift from pan with a slotted spoon and place in a deep 3-quart casserole.

Cut 2 to 2½ pounds **boneless beef stew** into about 2-inch chunks and sprinkle with **salt** and **pepper**.

Add meat to bacon drippings and cook on medium heat, stirring as needed, until meat is browned. With slotted spoon, transfer meat to casserole.

Add 6 to 8 small whole **onions** (about 1½-inch diameter) to frying pan and cook on medium heat until lightly browned, shaking pan to turn onions; lift from pan with a slotted spoon and set aside.

Blend 3 tablespoons **all-purpose flour** into drippings in frying pan; cook, stirring, until flour is golden. Remove from heat and stir in gradually 1½ cups **dry red wine**; 1 cup **regular-strength beef broth** or rich meat broth (page 16); 3 tablespoons **brandy**; 2 cloves **garlic**, minced or pressed; a 1 by 4-inch strip of **orange peel** (orange-colored part only, pared from fruit with a knife or vegetable peeler); and ½ teaspoon *each* **marjoram leaves** and **thyme leaves**. Bring to a boil, stirring; then pour over meat. Peel 1 medium-size **onion** and stick 6 **whole cloves** into it; tuck onion down into meat. Cover and bake in a 325° oven for 2½ hours.

Meanwhile, in same frying pan over medium-high heat, cook ½ pound small **mushrooms** (or quartered large mushrooms) in 2 tablespoons **butter** or margarine, stirring, until juices have evaporated; set aside.

When meat has baked 2½ hours, add small sautéed onions and mushrooms; push down into liquid, cover, and continue baking 15 minutes. Sprinkle with 2 tablespoons chopped **parsley**. Makes 6 to 8 servings.

Fillet of beef in a crust

(Boeuf en croûte)

A lavish entrée, this one is suited for entertaining since you can assemble it well ahead in steps that can be adjusted to busy schedules.

Because the shape of the roast will vary, directions tell you how to calculate the dimension of the pastry. The meat is encased in the pastry with a layer of cooked chopped mushrooms. You might sauté additional whole mushrooms and use them to decorate the roast when presented.

> 4-pound piece beef fillet
> 1 tablespoon butter or margarine, at room temperature
> Salt and pepper
> Rich pastry (directions page 57)
> Duxelles (directions page 57)
> 1 egg beaten with 1 tablespoon water
> Madeira sauce (directions page 57), Dijon mustard, or prepared horseradish
> Watercress or parsley sprigs

Have meatman trim most fat from fillet; then tie meat to form a compact, evenly shaped roast.

Place meat in a small, shallow baking pan and rub surface of roast with butter; then sprinkle lightly with salt and pepper.

Bake in a 425° oven for 30 minutes. Remove from oven and let cool; cover and chill until next day, if you like.

Measure length of the roast and diameter of widest section. Roll rich pastry out on a floured cloth, making a neat rectangle a little more than 5

(Continued on page 57)

. . . Fillet of beef in a crust (cont'd.)

inches longer than roast and 4 inches wider than diameter of roast; trim edges precisely with a knife and save pastry scraps.

Evenly spread duxelles on pastry in a rectangle the same size as meat dimensions; then press duxelles lightly but firmly with your palm to make a compact layer.

Center cold fillet on duxelles. Gently lift (do not pull) pastry up over length of meat; overlap pastry edges, compactly encasing meat; press pastry edges firmly together to seal. Fold in ends of pastry and seal (if there is an excessive accumulation of pastry in ends as you seal them, pinch out some of it so pastry is not much thicker than that wrapped around roast). Gently lift roll and place seam side down on an ungreased baking sheet.

Roll out scraps of dough on floured board; cut in decorative shapes and arrange on pastry-wrapped roast. Cover and chill as long as 6 hours.

Brush pastry with egg and water mixture. Bake in a 400° oven for 35 to 40 minutes or until pastry is richly browned.

BEEF FILLET IN CRUST is showy main course you can prepare ahead; bake just before serving and accompany thick slices with madeira-flavored sauce. Note assembling technique above.

SEAL COLD COOKED BEEF FILLET and duxelles of cooked mushrooms in pastry; decorate with fancifully cut pastry scraps.

Slip a spatula under pastry to make sure it is free; then carefully slide onto a serving platter and garnish with watercress or parsley.

With a very sharp knife, cut in slices about 1 inch thick (pastry breaks if you try to cut thin slices).

Serve roast with madeira sauce and/or Dijon mustard or prepared horseradish. Makes 8 to 10 servings.

Rich pastry. Cut 1½ cups (¾ lb.) **butter** or margarine in chunks and mix with 4 cups unsifted **all-purpose flour** and 1 teaspoon **salt**. Rub mixture with fingers (or mix, half at a time, in a food processor) until fine crumbs. With a fork, mix in 6 tablespoons **water**, sprinkling 1 tablespoon water over dough at a time and mixing lightly; stir until dough clings together. Shape into a compact ball. Chill, covered, as long as 4 days; use at room temperature.

Duxelles. Finely chop 1½ pounds **mushrooms**. Cook in ¼ cup **butter** or margarine in a wide frying pan over medium-high heat, stirring, until all liquid has evaporated and mushrooms are just beginning to brown. Add ¼ cup **madeira**, ½ cup chopped **shallots** or green onion, and ½ cup chopped **parsley**. Boil rapidly, stirring, until moisture is evaporated. Let cool before using; if made ahead, cover and chill until next day.

Madeira sauce. Chop 3 slices **bacon** and place in a wide frying pan. Add 2 medium-size **carrots**, minced; 1 small **onion**, minced; and ¼ cup minced **parsley**. Cook on medium-high heat, stirring, until vegetables are slightly soft and lightly browned. Warm ¼ cup **madeira**, set aflame, and pour into pan *(not beneath exhaust fan or flammable items)*; shake pan until flame dies. Set vegetables aside.

In a deep, small pan (about 1½-qt. size) combine 2 cans (14 oz. *each*) or 4 cups **regular-strength beef broth** or rich meat broth (page 16) and 3 **marrow-filled beef bones**, *each* about 3 inches long. Bring to a boil, reduce heat, and simmer 15 minutes. Lift bones from broth and, with a long slender knife or marrow spoon, ease marrow from bones; cut in chunks and set aside (chill, covered, if made ahead). Discard bone. Boil broth rapidly until reduced to 2 cups.

Stir 2 tablespoons **all-purpose flour** into vegetables; then gradually blend in 2 cups broth. Add 1 **bay leaf** and ½ teaspoon **thyme leaves**. Bring to a boil, stirring. (If made ahead, cover and chill; reheat to continue.) Gently mix marrow into hot sauce and add more **madeira** to taste, if desired. Serve hot.

Beef fillet with vegetable bouquet for two

(Chateaubriand à la bouquetière pour deux)

A deluxe cut of meat just the right size to be the basis of an elegant meal for two—that defines the thick center portion of the beef fillet, often called the "chateaubriand."

Chateaubriand with a vegetable bouquet, the way many fine restaurants present it, can be handled at home if you organize your time. A shallot butter, served alongside, flavors both meat and vegetables.

To bring all the food together easily for serving, you make the butter and cook the asparagus, onions, and carrots ahead, then reheat briefly. Keep the potatoes in the cooking water as long as an hour, mashing them while the meat broils.

> About 1¼-pound center section of
>   beef fillet
> Hot mashed potatoes (directions follow)
> Sugar-glazed carrots and onions, and fluted
>   mushrooms (directions follow)
> Asparagus (directions follow)
> Butter bercy (directions follow)

Trim, or have meatman trim, all fat from surface of fillet. With a flat-surfaced mallet, pound meat on a cut end until it is about 1¼ inches thick; tie string around sides if meat tends to pull apart.

Broil about 4 inches from heat for about 10 minutes on each side for rare (or broil to doneness you prefer).

Meanwhile, force mashed potatoes through a plain-tipped pastry bag, forming a decorative mound on a small carving board (or just spoon potatoes in a mound onto board). Cover surrounding areas of board with foil and broil potatoes about 2 inches from heat just until lightly touched with brown. (If you have only one oven, broil potatoes after steak, keeping meat warm in oven, below.)

Place meat on board; arrange carrots, onions, mushrooms, and asparagus alongside. Slice steak vertically and serve meat and vegetables with butter bercy. Makes 2 generous servings.

Hot mashed potatoes. Thoroughly blend into 1 to 1½ cups **unseasoned hot mashed potatoes** 1 tablespoon **butter** or margarine, 1 **egg yolk**, a dash of **grated nutmeg**, and sufficient **whipping cream** to give potatoes soft consistency; use warm.

Sugar-glazed carrots and onions, and fluted mushrooms. Peel 2 or 3 medium-size **carrots**, cut each in 2 or 3 even lengths, and then trim blunt ends to resemble small whole carrots. In covered pan, cook carrots and 3 or 4 small whole **onions** (about 1-inch diameter) together in **boiling salted water** to cover for 10 to 15 minutes or until easy to pierce. Drain; immerse in **ice water**. Drain, cover, and chill until next day if you like.

Cut stems flush with caps on 4 to 6 medium-size **mushrooms**. With small knife, gash or flute mushroom caps decoratively with shallow, evenly spaced cuts; set aside as long as 2 or 3 hours.

Melt 1 tablespoon **butter** or margarine in a small frying pan over medium heat. Add mushrooms and lightly brown; lift from pan and keep warm. Put drained carrots and onions in butter, adding ½ teaspoon **sugar**. Cook over high heat for 3 or 4 minutes, shaking pan to rotate and lightly brown vegetables as they heat. Serve hot.

Asparagus. Remove tough ends from 4 to 6 large **asparagus spears**; peel stems if desired. Cook, uncovered, in a single layer in a small shallow pan, with **boiling water** to cover, for about 6 minutes or just until barely tender when pierced. Drain and cover with **ice water**. Drain, cover, and chill until next day, if you like. To serve, cover with **boiling water** for 2 minutes; drain and serve hot.

Butter bercy. Boil 2 tablespoons **dry red wine** with 1 tablespoon minced **shallots** or red onion until wine is almost evaporated; cool. Blend well with ¼ cup room-temperature **butter** or margarine, 1 tablespoon minced **parsley**, and 1 teaspoon **lemon juice**. Serve at room temperature.

Basic steak sauté

(Steak sauté)

A great many of the French ways with a steak begin in the frying pan and go very quickly, as you cook on high heat. Considerable variety is achieved in the finishing steps. The following entrées range from supersimple to grandly styled, but they all begin with this basic sauté step.

For 4 to 6 servings, select tender **boneless beef steaks** cut 1 to 1½ inches thick, allowing ⅓ to ½ pound per person. Use a cut from rib, loin, or fillet, or use a single, whole flank steak (1½ to 1¾ lb.) or 2 to 3 whole skirt steaks (¾ lb. each —keep steaks flat; do not roll or tenderize). Trim off excess fat or score fat to prevent meat from curling as it cooks.

In a wide frying pan over medium-high heat, melt 1 tablespoon **butter** or margarine with 1 tablespoon **olive oil** or salad oil.

Add meat and cook, uncovered, until well browned on each side; allow 3 to 5 minutes a side for rare meat or cook to doneness you prefer.

At this point you can season meat with **salt** and **pepper** and serve, or season according to one of the recipes that follow. Makes 4 to 6 servings.

French hamburgers

Along the Champs Élysées and other busy boulevards of Paris, bistros post their menus for perusal by passersby. They offer all manner of food—including the hamburger.

Indeed, that familiar ground meat patty, browned and juicy and at the heart of many a meal, becomes something special when the French determine what goes in, on, or over it.

Beef patties. For 4 broiled beef patties, divide 1½ pounds **lean ground beef** equally in fourths; shape into ½-inch-thick patties. Broil on a rack 3 inches from heat until cooked to your liking; allow 4 minutes on each side for rare meat. Sprinkle with **salt** to taste. Garnish according to one of the recipes that follow and serve hot.

Hamburger niçoise

(Hamburger à la niçoise)

A crisscross of anchovies and an olive adorn the meat, emphasizing the south-of-France flavors. Ratatouille, a cold vegetable stew, is the accompaniment. Serve with butter and crusty rolls.

- 4 **hot broiled beef patties (see preceding directions)**
- 8 **canned anchovy fillets**
- 4 **pitted ripe olives**
  Ratatouille (page 68)
  Butter lettuce leaves

Place each beef patty on a serving plate and lay 2 anchovies on top, crossing them over center of patty; put an olive at their intersection. Spoon an equal amount of ratatouille onto each plate and garnish with lettuce leaves. Makes 4 servings.

Tarragon burger

(Hamburger à l'estragon)

If you like, use the herb butter not only to top the hot beef but also on boiled new potatoes.

- ½ **teaspoon tarragon leaves**
- 1 **tablespoon vinegar**
- 4 **tablespoons room-temperature butter or margarine**
- 2 **tablespoons minced parsley**
- 4 **hot broiled beef patties (see preceding directions)**

In a small pan, combine tarragon and vinegar; boil just until liquid is almost gone. Set aside until cooled slightly; then scrape all tarragon into butter; add parsley and blend. Use at room temperature or cold; cover to chill.

Divide butter equally and place each portion atop a hot beef patty. Makes 4 servings.

Hamburgers with eggs on horseback

(Hamburgers avec oeufs à cheval)

First, pan-fry hashed brown potatoes until crisply browned; then keep them warm as the meat patties broil and eggs cook.

- About 4 **tablespoons butter or margarine**
- 2 **packages (12 oz. *each*) frozen hashed brown potatoes**
- 4 **hot broiled beef patties (see preceding directions)**
- 4 **hot cooked eggs (fried or poached)**
  Salt and pepper

Melt 4 tablespoons butter in a wide frying pan. Add frozen potato patties and cook over medium-high heat, turning occasionally with a spatula, until well browned; add more butter if needed to prevent sticking. Transfer potato patties to 4 individual serving plates, set a beef patty on each potato mound, and then place an egg on each serving of beef. Season with salt and pepper. Makes 4 servings.

Steak with green peppercorn sauce
(Steak au poivre vert)

The tangy green peppercorns you purchase canned (in salt water or vinegar) or freeze-dried distinguish this popular steak dish.

Cook your choice of **steak** for 4 to 6 servings according to basic sauté directions (page 58). When meat is cooked, add to pan 6 tablespoons **brandy** and set aflame (*not under an exhaust fan or flammable items*), shaking pan until flame dies. Transfer meat to a serving dish and keep warm.

To pan add ¼ to ½ cup minced **shallots** or onion and stir on high heat for 2 or 3 minutes, or just until soft.

Measure 1 or 2 tablespoons canned or freeze-dried **green peppercorns** into a strainer; quickly rinse in **cold water** and drain.

Add green peppercorns to pan along with ¾ cup **whipping cream** or creme fraîche (page 77), 1 tablespoon **Dijon mustard**, and ½ teaspoon **tarragon leaves**. Boil on high heat for 3 to 4 minutes, stirring, until shiny bubbles form (drain any accumulated steak juices into cream, also). **Salt** meat to taste and pour sauce over. If steak is a flank, thinly slice at an angle across grain before topping with sauce. Makes 4 to 6 servings.

Steak with meat glaze
(Steak à la glace de viande)

Superlative is an adequate description of the results when steak is paired with this intensely flavored (but not calorie rich), clinging meat glaze.

Meat glaze, made from greatly reduced broth, can be stored in the freezer in premeasured portions. The initial production of the glaze takes time, but if you have it on hand, this dish is very easy to put together.

Brown **steak** for 4 servings as directed for basic steak sauté (page 58). When steaks are removed from frying pan, turn heat high and add ¼ cup minced **shallots** or onions (optional), ¼ cup **madeira**, and ¼ cup **meat glaze** (page 16).

Heat, stirring to free any browned particles, until boiling; add any steak juices to pan. Pour sauce over meat, slice, and serve. Makes 4 servings.

PUNGENTLY FLAVORED green peppercorns speckle creamy sauce that is quickly made. After sautéing flank steak, prepare sauce, spoon onto thinly sliced meat, and serve with cooked spinach and tiny buttered carrots.

Steak with marrow sauce
(Steak à la moelle)

If you like marrow, you'll find its addition to meat glaze makes a sauce that is hard to surpass.

Prepare meat for 4 servings as directed for **steak with meat glaze** (left), adding **marrow** (directions follow) along with **madeira** and **meat glaze**. Spoon sauce over meat. Makes 4 servings.

Marrow. Place 3 **beef marrow bones**, *each* 3½ inches long, in a small, deep pan (about 1½-qt. size); add **regular-strength chicken broth** or beef broth, or rich meat broth (page 16) up to about half the depth of the bones. Cover and simmer about 20 minutes or until marrow looks translucent. Let cool slightly; then push marrow from bones or ease out with a knife or marrow spoon; cut in chunks. If prepared ahead, cover and chill. Save broth for other uses.

Steak with wine glaze
(Steak marchand de vin)

An everyday way with steak that is popular in bistros and cafés bears frequent repetition.

Cook your choice of **steak** for 4 to 6 servings according to basic steak sauté directions (page 58).

When steaks are cooked, set aside and keep warm. Add to pan 2 tablespoons **butter** or margarine and 6 tablespoons chopped **shallots** or red onion. Cook shallots, uncovered, on medium-high heat, stirring, until they are soft but not browned.

Pour into pan ½ cup **dry red wine** and boil, stirring, over high heat until most liquid is gone.

Spoon sauce onto steaks. Makes 4 to 6 servings.

Steak with black pepper
(Steak au poivre)

More pungently seasoned than steak with green peppercorns, steak with black peppers is less richly finished.

Select **steaks** for 4 servings, cut 1 inch thick, as directed for basic steak sauté (page 58); do not use flank or skirt steak.

Coarsely crush about 2 teaspoons **whole black peppers** (or use 2 teaspoons cracked black pepper). Spread pepper out on a flat surface and turn meat in pepper, pressing to pick up all. Then, with your hand, press peppers firmly into meat.

Cook steaks as directed for basic steak sauté; remove from pan and keep hot.

To pan add 2 tablespoons minced **shallots** or green onion and cook, stirring, on high heat just until shallots are soft. Pour in 6 tablespoons **cognac** or brandy and set aflame at once (*not under an exhaust fan or flammable items*); shake pan until flame dies; then add ¼ cup **dry red wine** or regular-strength beef broth or rich meat broth (page 16) to pan. Stir to free any browned bits and pour sauce over meat to serve. Makes 4 servings.

Steak with mustard sauce
(Steak à la sauce moutarde)

The juices of the cut, cooked steak become an integral part of the sauce.

Prepare **basic steak sauté** (page 58) for 4 to 6 servings, using a large cut, such as rib, loin, or flank; keep warm on a serving platter.

In a small pan, melt 3 or 4 tablespoons **butter** or margarine over medium heat. Stirring briskly, blend in 1 tablespoon **Dijon mustard**, 2 tablespoons **dry vermouth** or dry white wine, and ¼ teaspoon **Worcestershire**. Pour sauce over steak. Slice meat and swirl through juices; then spoon steak and juices onto serving plates. Makes 4 to 6 servings.

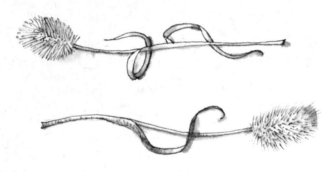

Steak sauté with onions
(Onglet sauté aux oignons)

Full-flavored skirt steaks teamed with an abundance of amber-toned onions yield a hearty but well-balanced combination. The onions must be slowly cooked to develop their rich, mellow potential, but this is a step you can complete hours, even days, in advance.

To finish the dish, brown the steaks, set aside, and reheat the onions with some additional seasonings in the pan juices.

Select 2 or 3 **skirt steaks** (*each* about ¾ lb.) and trim off excess fat. If desired, cut meat in serving-size pieces. Cook as directed for basic steak sauté

(page 58); these steaks are thin and fill pan more than thicker cuts, so you may have to cook pieces in sequence. Keep cooked meat warm as balance is being sautéed.

When all meat is cooked, transfer to a serving dish and put in a warm place. Add to frying pan 1 recipe's worth **slow-cooked onions** (page 66), 2 tablespoons **wine vinegar**, and ¼ cup chopped **parsley**. Bring to boiling over high heat, stirring. Spoon onions onto meat; season with **salt** and **pepper**. Makes 4 to 6 servings.

Beef fillet Rossini
(Tournedos Rossini)

Delightfully elaborate—for an occasion when you want to show off, yet haven't much time—fillets Rossini are elegantly garnished with canned liver pâté, artichoke bottoms, and truffles (which are optional).

Have chilled 1 can (about 8 oz., or smaller cans of total equivalent) **pâté de foie**.

Rapidly boil 1 cup **regular-strength beef broth** or rich meat broth (page 16) and ¼ cup **madeira** until reduced to about ½ cup. Blend ½ teaspoon **cornstarch** with 2 teaspoons **water** and stir into sauce; bring to a boil, stirring; set aside.

Cut ends from pâté cans and push out chilled pâté; cut into 6 equal slices and arrange side by side on a baking sheet; cover with foil. Heat in 325° oven for 10 minutes.

Select 6 small, equal-size **beef fillet steaks**, *each* cut 1 inch thick. Cook according to directions for basic steak sauté (page 58).

Meanwhile, heat 6 canned **artichoke bottoms** (3-inch-diameter size) in their own liquid in a small pan.

To serve, arrange drained artichoke bottoms on a warm serving platter or individual dishes; set a cooked fillet on each artichoke, then top meat with a slice of warm pâté. If desired, lay a thin slice of canned **truffle** on each piece of pâté.

Heat sauce to simmering and spoon an equal amount onto each steak. Makes 6 servings.

Beef fillets Héloïse
(Tournedos Héloïse)

To convert tournedos Rossini to tournedos Héloïse, add mushrooms cooked in cream.

Prepare **mushrooms boiled with cream** (page 66). Prepare **beef fillet Rossini** (preceding) and arrange on a serving platter; spoon mushrooms alongside meat. Makes 6 servings.

Vegetables and salads

"Eat with the seasons."

Vegetables are the chameleons of French cookery. They change their role (though not their color), fitting into different niches of the menu with complete adaptability.

In one chapter, vegetables appear as appetizers. In another, they are the backbone of many a fine soup. In the main-dish chapters, they contribute their seasoning strengths to dishes of fish, shellfish, poultry, rabbit, and meats; sometimes the vegetables are an integral part of the classical styling of a dish—like navarin.

In this chapter are vegetables to serve with the main dish. Leg of lamb on Sunday in France is incomplete unless accompanied by boiled beans; a handsome roast might be flanked attractively by tomatoes gratin and carrots vichy; creamed sorrel is a lively complement for veal roast; and in

asparagus with salmon, both vegetable and fish benefit mutually by the addition of hollandaise.

Good cooks like to capitalize on pairing plainly cooked vegetables with well-sauced entrées, letting the vegetables share the enrichments. In reverse, the good cook also likes to team well-seasoned vegetables with simply cooked entrées, or perhaps make them a first course—for example, artichokes florentine, chestnut soufflé, or leeks with tarragon. They are all here.

Directions for growing sorrel, a green that flourishes in most climates and is savored by the French, are in this chapter.

Also included are sauces that complement a wide range of vegetables and other foods: bechamel and mornay, plus the tricky ones—hollandaise, mayonnaise, and their variations. You'll learn what makes these sauces work and, more importantly, how to turn a failure into success.

Salad in the French meal follows the entrée, and its function is to refresh the palate. In this placement, salad means greens with a dressing. The dressings offered here are quite representative of those served in France.

Cheese can follow the salad, but in most French homes, for day-to-day dining, the cheese accompanies the salad. Suggested are cheeses you can buy to give the French touch.

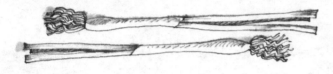

Artichokes florentine
(Artichauts florentins)

You will need 6 to 8 **cooked artichoke bottoms** (*each* 2 or 3 inches in diameter). Use drained canned or thawed frozen artichoke bottoms.

Arrange artichoke bottoms side by side in a shallow casserole (about 1½-qt. size). Cover artichokes with 1 recipe's worth **creamed spinach** (page 68); then spoon 1 recipe's worth **mornay sauce** (page 70) over spinach. Sprinkle with ½ cup shredded **Gruyère cheese** or Parmesan cheese. (At this point you can cover and chill until next day.)

Bake, uncovered, in a 375° oven for 30 minutes or until bubbly (40 minutes if chilled). Makes 6 to 8 servings.

Asparagus, hot or cold with sauces
(Asperges)

Allow 1 pound **asparagus** for 2 or 3 servings. Wash well and snap off tough ends. If desired, peel stalks with a vegetable peeler.

Lay spears parallel, no more than 2 or 3 layers deep, in a wide frying pan in **boiling salted water** to cover. Cook over high heat, uncovered, for 6 to 8 minutes or until stems are just tender when pierced. Drain at once.

To serve asparagus hot, spoon on **melted butter**, hollandaise (page 69), béarnaise (page 70), mousseline sauce (page 70), or mornay sauce (page 70). Allow 1 to 3 tablespoons sauce for a serving.

To serve asparagus cold, immerse drained vegetable in **ice water** just until chilled. Drain and keep cold and covered until ready to serve—as long as next day. Accompany with **mayonnaise** (page 69), housewife's dressing (page 71), or any of the sauces mentioned above, except melted butter or mornay sauce.

Carrots vichy
(Carottes à la vichy)

Peel 8 to 12 slender **carrots**. Lay flat in a wide frying pan in **boiling salted water** to cover. Cook, covered, at simmer 15 to 20 minutes or until carrots are just easy to pierce. Drain off liquid.

Add to pan 4 tablespoons **butter** or margarine and 2 tablespoons **cognac** or brandy (optional) and cook on medium-high heat, shaking pan until carrots are lightly browned. Mix in ¼ cup minced **parsley** and sprinkle with **salt** to taste. Makes 4 to 6 servings.

Cauliflower mornay
(Chou-fleur mornay)

Break 1 medium-size **cauliflower** (about 1¼ lb.) into flowerets. Cook in **boiling salted water** to cover, with lid on, for 10 to 15 minutes or just until tender when pierced.

Drain and place in a shallow casserole (about 1½-qt. size).

Spoon 1 recipe's worth **mornay sauce** (page 70) evenly over vegetable. Sprinkle with ½ cup shredded **Swiss cheese** and broil 4 inches from heat to brown lightly.

Or omit broiling; cover and chill until next day. Then bake, uncovered, in a 375° oven for about 30 minutes or until sauce is bubbling. Makes 4 servings.

Chestnut soufflé
(Soufflé aux marrons)

In a wide frying pan over medium heat, cook 1 medium-size **carrot**, coarsely shredded, and 2 medium-size **onions**, chopped, in 2 tablespoons **butter** or margarine until vegetables are soft, stirring occasionally.

Remove from heat and add 1 can (15½ oz.) **unsweetened chestnut purée**, 3 tablespoons **port**, 4 **egg yolks**, and ½ teaspoon **salt**. Beat until well blended.

Measure ½ cup **sliced almonds** and set aside 2 tablespoons; stir remaining nuts into purée mixture.

Beat 4 **egg whites** until they hold firm, moist peaks; then gently fold into purée mixture. Pour into a well-buttered shallow casserole or soufflé dish (about 1½-qt. size). Sprinkle with reserved almonds.

Bake, uncovered, in a 350° oven until top is just firm (about 40 minutes for shallow casserole, 55 minutes for soufflé dish). Serve with additional **melted butter**, if desired. Makes 6 to 8 servings.

Green beans with sauces
(Haricots verts)

Allow 1 pound **green beans** for 3 or 4 servings. Snap ends and pull any strings from beans; wash and drain. Cook, uncovered, in **boiling salted water** to cover for about 8 to 10 minutes or just until beans are tender when pierced (more mature beans may take as long as 20 minutes).

Drain and serve hot with **melted butter**, hollandaise (page 69), béarnaise (page 70), or mousseline sauce (page 70), allowing 2 to 3 tablespoons sauce for a serving.

"Wash well the vegetables".

Green beans gratin
(Haricots verts gratinés)

Mince 1 small **onion**. Prepare **béchamel sauce** (page 70), cooking onion in the **butter** until soft before adding remaining ingredients; set aside.

Cook 2 pounds **green beans** according to preceding directions. Drain and place in a shallow casserole (about 1½-qt. size).

Heat sauce to simmering, stirring; then pour over beans. Sprinkle with ½ cup shredded **Swiss cheese** or Gruyère cheese and broil 4 inches from heat until cheese melts. Makes 6 to 8 servings.

Green beans polonaise
(Haricots verts à la polonaise)

Cook 2 pounds **green beans** according to preceding directions.

While they cook, melt 6 tablespoons **butter** or margarine in a small frying pan. Add ½ cup **fine dry bread crumbs** and cook on medium heat, stirring, until toasted. Mix in 2 tablespoons minced **parsley**.

Also finely chop whites of 2 **hard-cooked eggs** and force yolks through a wire strainer; keep separate.

Drain beans and place in serving dish. Top with crumbs, egg white, then yolk. Drizzle with 2 tablespoons **melted butter**. Makes 6 to 8 servings.

Boiled white beans
(Haricots blancs)

Sort through 1 pound (2 cups) **dried small white beans**, picking out any extraneous materials. Rinse and drain beans and place in a 4-quart pan. Add 8 cups **water** (or regular-strength chicken or beef broth, or rich meat broth, page 16), 6 to 8 whole large **shallots** (about 1 cup), 1 **bay leaf**, 1 teaspoon

thyme leaves, 6 to 8 **parsley** sprigs, and 1 medium-size **carrot**, finely chopped.

Cover and bring to a boil; then reduce heat and simmer for 2½ hours or until beans have a creamy texture when bitten; stir occasionally. Discard parsley. (If cooked ahead, chill and cover; reheat to serve, adding **water** if needed.) Add **salt** to taste. Makes about 6 cups or 6 to 8 servings.

Boiled flageolets
(Flageolets)

Use **dried flageolets** (pale green beans about same size as small white beans). Follow directions for boiled white beans (preceding), but reduce water to 7 cups and omit carrot. Cook for 2 hours or until beans have a creamy texture when bitten. Makes 6 cups or 6 to 8 servings.

Leeks with tarragon
(Poireaux à l'estragon)

Trim and clean 2 pounds (about 6 to 8) medium-size **leeks** in this manner: trim root end, remove tough fibrous outer layers, and trim off tough green leaves, leaving tender-looking portions.

Split leeks lengthwise. Hold each section under running water and flip layers to rinse away any soil.

Lay leeks parallel into about 1 inch **boiling salted water**; cover and simmer 10 to 15 minutes or until stem ends are tender to pierce. Lift leeks gently from water, preserving shape, and place on a serving dish.

Melt 2 tablespoons **butter** or margarine and stir in 1 tablespoon chopped **parsley**, ¼ teaspoon **tarragon leaves**, and ¼ cup grated **Parmesan cheese**. Spoon over leeks. Makes 4 to 6 servings.

Braised leeks
(Poireaux braisés)

Cook **leeks** according to preceding directions. Season with **butter**, **salt**, and **pepper**. Omit parsley, tarragon leaves, and cheese. Makes 4 to 6 servings.

Mushrooms boiled with cream
(Champignons à la crème)

In a wide frying pan over medium heat, simmer 1 pound sliced **mushrooms**, ¼ cup minced **shallots** or onion (optional), and 1 cup **crème fraîche** (page 77) or whipping cream, stirring occasionally, for about 5 minutes or until mushrooms start to give up juices.

Then turn heat to high and boil, uncovered, stirring frequently, for about 10 minutes or until liquid is reduced to a shiny sauce and big bubbles form. Stir in 1 to 3 tablespoons minced **parsley** and **salt** to taste. Serve mushrooms as a vegetable dish or spooned onto **toast** as an appetizer. Makes 4 vegetable servings or 4 to 6 first-course servings.

Onions with meat glaze
(Oignons à la glace de viande)

Place 12 to 18 very small whole **onions** (1 to 1½-inch diameter) in a wide frying pan with 2 tablespoons **butter** or margarine and ½ cup **regular-strength chicken broth** or beef broth, or rich meat broth (page 16).

Cover and cook over medium-low heat for about 10 minutes or until broth evaporates; then continue cooking, shaking pan occasionally, for about 10 minutes or until onions are lightly browned. Add 3 to 4 tablespoons **meat glaze** (page 16) and bring to a boil, shaking pan. Add **salt** to taste. Makes 4 to 6 servings.

Slow-cooked onions
(Oignons braisés)

Melt 2 tablespoons **butter** or margarine in a wide frying pan over medium heat. Slice 3 large **onions** and separate into rings; add to butter. Cook, stirring often, for about 20 minutes or until onions become very soft and begin to develop a golden color. Add **salt** to taste. Serve hot (can be made ahead, chilled, and reheated.) Use as is or stir in ¾ cup **crème fraîche** (page 77) or sour cream. Serve as a vegetable or as a topping for other vegetables, such as asparagus, green beans, or cauliflower. Makes about 1 cup or 4 servings.

Glazed parsnips
(Panais glacés)

Cook 8 to 12 (about 1 lb.) medium-size **parsnips** in **boiling salted water** to cover in a wide frying pan (so parsnips lie flat), with lid on, for 10 to 15 minutes or until easy to pierce.

Drain off liquid and add to pan 3 tablespoons **butter** or margarine. Cook on medium heat for 10 to 15 minutes or until parsnips are lightly browned; shake pan to turn vegetables. Add **salt** to taste.

If desired, add 3 tablespoons **whipping cream**. Turn heat high; boil until cream is reduced about half, shaking pan constantly. Makes 4 servings.

Peas with lettuce
(Petits pois aux laitues)

In a large frying pan over high heat melt ¼ cup **butter** or margarine; add 3 cups shredded **iceberg lettuce** and cook, stirring, for 2 to 3 minutes or until wilted. At once stir in 2 packages (10 oz. *each*) thawed frozen **petite peas**; ¼ cup minced **parsley**; ½ teaspoon **sugar**; and ⅛ teaspoon **ground nutmeg** and cook until peas are heated and liquid is boiling. Add **salt** to taste. Makes 6 to 8 servings.

Potatoes gratin
(Pommes de terre gratinées)

For *each* serving, allow 1 **new potato** (about ¾ lb.). Peel and thinly slice into a shallow individual baking dish (about 1½-cup size); level potatoes and sprinkle lightly with **salt** and **pepper**. Pour in **whipping cream** to barely cover potatoes (about ⅓ cup).

Bake, uncovered, in a 325° oven for 1 hour or until tender when pierced. Sprinkle with ¼ cup shredded **Swiss cheese** or Gruyère cheese and bake 3 or 4 minutes more or until cheese melts.

To make 4 to 5 servings of potatoes gratin, follow preceding directions but use a shallow 1½-quart casserole, 4 to 5 cups thinly sliced **new potatoes** (about 2 lbs.), **salt**, about 1 cup **whipping cream** (or use half cream and half regular-strength chicken or beef broth, or rich meat broth, page 16) or enough to barely cover potatoes.

Bake, uncovered, for about 1 hour and 20 minutes. After 1 hour, sprinkle on potatoes ¾ cup shredded **Swiss cheese** or Gruyère cheese.

VEGETABLES, FRENCH-STYLE, from lower left, up, include peas with lettuce, carrots vichy, leeks with tarragon, vegetable stew (ratatouille), glazed parsnips, green beans polonaise, potatoes gratin, onions with meat glaze, and (center) mushrooms boiled with cream.

Pilaf
(Pilaf)

In a 2 to 3-quart pan over medium heat, melt 4 tablespoons **butter** or margarine. Add 1 **onion**, chopped, and 1 clove **garlic**, minced or pressed. Cook, stirring, until onion is limp (about 5 minutes). Add 1 cup **long grain white rice** and continue to cook, stirring, for 5 to 10 minutes or until grains are lightly toasted and look opaque.

Pour in 2 cups **regular-strength chicken broth**, or beef broth, or rich meat broth (page 16). Bring to boiling, cover, reduce heat, and simmer for about 20 minutes or until rice is tender; stir once or twice. Add **salt** to taste. Serve as is or stir in ¼ cup shredded **Parmesan cheese**. Serves 4.

Creamed sorrel
(Oseille à la crème)

Tear out and discard stem and center rib of **sorrel leaves** if tough. Wash leaves well and drain.

To cook 1 pound sorrel leaves (about 10 cups, lightly packed) bring 4 quarts **water** to boiling. Drop leaves into water and push beneath surface. (Leaves turn a very drab green as soon as heated.) Drain at once and cover leaves with cold water; this minimizes acid level. Drain well; at this point sorrel can be covered and chilled until next day.

In a pan, mix sorrel with 1 recipe's worth **béchamel sauce** (page 70) and heat, stirring, uncovered until bubbling. Add **salt** to taste. Makes 4 or 5 servings.

Creamed spinach
(Épinards à la crème)

Place tender, well-washed and drained leaves from 2 pounds **spinach** in a large pan. Cover and cook over low heat for 3 or 4 minutes in **water** that clings to leaves until just wilted, stirring once or twice. Drain well and chop; you should have about 2 cups (or use 2 cups frozen, thawed, drained chopped spinach).

Blend with 1 recipe's worth **béchamel sauce** (page 70); heat through, stirring. Makes 4 servings.

Tomatoes gratin
(Tomates gratinées)

Cut 4 firm, medium-size **tomatoes** (peeled, if desired) in half horizontally and gently squeeze out seeds. Mix together ½ cup **fine dry bread crumbs**; 1 clove **garlic**, minced or pressed; ¼ cup **melted butter** or olive oil; and 3 tablespoons minced **parsley**.

Set tomatoes, cut side up, side by side in a shallow casserole. Spoon crumb mixture evenly onto tomatoes, then press to compact slightly.

Bake in a 400° oven for 15 minutes or until tomatoes are hot. Makes 4 to 8 servings.

Vegetable stew
(Ratatouille)

In a wide frying pan over medium heat, combine 3 tablespoons **olive oil** or salad oil; 1 small **onion**, chopped; and 1 clove **garlic**, minced or pressed. Cook, stirring, until limp.

Add 1 medium-size (about 1 lb.) **eggplant**, cut in 1-inch cubes; 2 medium-size **zucchini**, cut in 1-inch slices; 1 can (1 lb.) **tomatoes** (chop up with spoon), including liquid; 1 teaspoon **basil leaves**; and ½ teaspoon **salt**.

Bring to a boil, reduce heat, cover, and simmer for about 35 minutes or until eggplant is very soft; stir occasionally. Uncover and boil rapidly about 20 minutes, stirring often, until most liquid evaporates. **Salt** to taste.

Serve hot, reheated, or at room temperature. To store (as long as a week), cover and chill. Garnish, if desired, with **sliced tomatoes** and **parsley sprigs**. Makes 4 to 6 servings.

Ratatouille in the oven. The vegetables hold their shape best when baked, but they take longer to cook. Mix **vegetables** and **olive oil** for **ratatouille** (preceding), in a 3-quart casserole.

Cover and bake in a 400° oven for 2 hours or until eggplant is very soft; stir once or twice.

Emulsion sauces

The classic French emulsion sauces—mayonnaise, hollandaise, and their many flavor variations—have a bad reputation. They're supposed to be tricky to make and easy to spoil. But the truth is that when you know how to make one sauce work, the others are a snap.

What is an emulsion? It's a liquid mixture in which minute drops of fat (that normally want to join together) are held apart in the liquid by a complex thing called an "emulsifier." Milk and cream are natural emulsions; so is egg yolk. In the case of the sauces, the emulsifier is mostly egg, but mustard (added for flavor, too) also helps the emulsion to form.

The trick to making an emulsion sauce is to break liquid fat into droplets by mixing, while at the same time working these droplets into the natural emulsion of the egg yolk—which then keeps the droplets apart.

You find hundreds of recipes for making mayonnaise, hollandaise, and their variations. The proportions that follow for each make sauces that are thick, highly stable, and good tasting.

Do these sauces freeze? You can successfully freeze and rewarm hollandaise and béarnaise made from these recipes. The mayonnaise breaks when thawed, but can be reemulsified easily.

Frozen and unfrozen butter sauces act the same: when reheated both are inclined to liquefy, but can be speedily reemulsified. Béarnaise, because of seasoning particles, is more stable.

To rewarm butter sauces, first bring to room temperature and stir to soften.

To heat further, set container in water just warm to touch; mix constantly with a fork. Transfer to water that's hot to touch; stir with a whip until sauce is slightly warmed.

How to fix a curdled sauce. To rescue about 1 cup of **sauce** (or 1 recipe's worth), put 1 tablespoon **water** (hot or cold) in a bowl. With a whip or a fork, beat a tiny stream of broken sauce into water —new droplets of fat are formed and held apart, and emulsifier can go back to work. Keep adding curdled sauce slowly, as when making original sauce, until all ingredients are incorporated and emulsion is reestablished.

If using a blender or food processor, first whip enough broken sauce into water to make about ¼ cup liquid. Put this in blender and whirl at high speed, slowly adding sauce to form new emulsion.

Mayonnaise (*Mayonnaise*). Use ingredients at room temperature and serve mayonnaise at room temperature or chilled. For the fluffiest, foamiest mayonnaise with the most volume, use a whole egg and beat with a whip or rotary beater. For a thicker, stiffer sauce that is more golden in color and richer in flavor, use all egg yolks. Your taste determines your choice.

By adding vinegar or lemon in sequence while blending in the oil, you get a thicker mayonnaise than when all the acid is added at the start.

Put 1 **egg** or 3 egg yolks, 1 teaspoon **Dijon mustard** or other mustard, and 1 teaspoon **wine vinegar** or lemon juice in mixing container. Beat at high speed (with whip, rotary beater, blender or food processor) until well blended.

Add 1 cup **salad oil** (may be part olive oil), mixing in just a few drops at a time at first, then increasing flow to a slow, steady stream about ¹⁄₁₆ inch wide.

Particularly with a blender or food processor, the slower the addition of oil, the thicker the sauce will be (up to a point—you can break the emulsion if the friction of the machine, on long mixing, creates too much heat).

As emulsion forms, mixture becomes opaque and starts to thicken. When ½ the oil is added, add 1 more teaspoon **wine vinegar**, then continue to mix as you add balance of oil. Add 1 more teaspoon **wine vinegar**. Cover sauce and chill until ready to use (as long as 10 days). Makes 1 to 1½ cups, depending upon mixing method.

Watercress mayonnaise (*Mayonnaise au cresson*). Follow the technique for making **mayonnaise** (left), but add all the acid in the beginning and use a blender or food processor.

In a blender or food processor, combine 1 **egg** or 3 egg yolks, 3 tablespoons **wine vinegar** or lemon juice, 3 tablespoons chopped **parsley**, 2 coarsely chopped **green onions** (with some tops), ½ cup packed **watercress leaves**, and ¼ teaspoon **tarragon leaves**. Whirl until fairly smooth; then add 1 cup **salad oil** as directed in mayonnaise recipe. Makes about 2 cups.

Hollandaise (*Sauce hollandaise*). The sauce is made with hot melted butter or margarine and may or

Growing sorrel for the kitchen
(Comment cultiver l'oseille)

Scarcely known in this country, sorrel is a staple in French cooking, under the name of "oseille." To botanists it is *Rumex scutatus*, a species of dock.

It tastes like a sharp, sprightly spinach but is a much better performer in the garden. A perennial, it will bear for many years. It is indifferent to heat, and in mild-winter climates (such as in some parts of the West) it produces leaves all year. (The plants go dormant in winter where the ground freezes, but revive earlier than other vegetables.)

Sorrel seeds and plants are not easy to find; search the herb sections of nurseries, seed racks, or catalogs. Plant seeds in spring, as early as possible without risk of frost damage; sow thinly in ¼-inch-deep rows that are 18 inches apart. Thin seedlings to 8 inches apart in the rows.

Nursery plants, where obtainable, are usually in 2-inch plant bands. Set them out in spring; divide the following spring to increase your supply. A dozen plants supply sorrel for a family of four.

Plants thrive in ordinary good garden soil and will tolerate more shade than most vegetables. Occasional light feeding will increase leaf growth; deep watering on a regular basis is necessary.

Groom plants by pulling off old, yellow leaves and by pinching off flower stalks that form in midsummer. If plants become crowded after 2 or 3 years, dig and divide in spring, replanting the divisions in enriched soil.

Before using, clean sorrel well. Tear off and discard stem and center rib, if tough; wash leaves.

may not be cooked. Heat affects the egg in some complex ways: it thickens the sauce; it also makes the egg less effective as an emulsifier so it is easier for fat droplets to rejoin, causing the sauce to break.

Flavor and texture distinguish a cooked sauce from an uncooked one. Adding acid in sequence has no thickening effect. An all-yolk sauce will be thicker, more golden, and richer tasting than a whole-egg sauce, regardless of how they are made. All are good—it's a matter of preference. When butter sauces cool, they thicken as fat congeals.

Put 1 **egg** or 3 egg yolks, 1 teaspoon **Dijon mustard** or other mustard, and 1 tablespoon **lemon juice** or wine vinegar in mixing container and mix until well blended.

If you are using a blender or food processor, add 1 cup **melted butter** or margarine at the same rate described for adding oil for mayonnaise (page 69). Serve at once; or if sauce is to be used within several hours, leave at room temperature, then reheat. If made farther ahead, cover and chill up to 1 week; let come to room temperature before trying to warm (directions, page 69).

If you are using a rotary beater or whip, follow this procedure: place egg mixture above gently **simmering water** and beat in butter at same rate described for adding oil for mayonnaise (page 69). (Best mixing container is a round-bottom bowl that will nest above water in a saucepan. Straight sides of some double boilers make it hard to keep all sauce well mixed—and if just some of it starts to melt, all sauce will liquefy.)

Once emulsion forms you can add fat more quickly than when using a blender. If you add it too slowly, you may end up with scrambled egg and a broken sauce. Continue to cook and beat after fat is added until sauce thickens—egg cooks a bit.

A cooked whole-egg sauce will look like cream that is just beginning to thicken when whipped; an all-yolk sauce will be thick enough to hold its shape briefly if dropped from a beater. Remove at once from heat when cooked, and serve or store as directed for blender-made sauce. Makes 1 to 1½ cups sauce, depending on mixing method.

Béarnaise (*Sauce béarnaise*). Simmer 1 tablespoon minced **shallots** or onion and ½ teaspoon **tarragon leaves** in 2 tablespoons **wine vinegar**, stirring, until liquid evaporates. Prepare **hollandaise** as directed (above), adding shallot mixture (use hot or cold) with **egg**, **mustard**, and **lemon juice**. Makes 1 to 1½ cups.

CHEERY MARKET VENDOR in Sarlat, France, offers produce from his own farm, including figs, tomatoes, squash, beans, radishes, cabbage, parsnips, greens, onions, and other foods familiar to our kitchens.

Mousseline sauce (*Sauce mousseline*). When you are ready to serve **hollandaise** (left), fold in ½ cup **whipping cream** that is whipped stiff. Serve at once. Makes about 2 cups. (To make 1 cup sauce, use ¼ cup **whipping cream** and about ½ cup **hollandaise**.)

Cooked sauces

Both sauces are simple, well-seasoned variations of the old standard white sauce.

Béchamel sauce (*Sauce béchamel*). Melt 2 tablespoons **butter** or margarine in a small pan over medium heat. Mix in 2 tablespoons **all-purpose flour** and cook, stirring, until flour is light golden color.

Remove from heat and blend in ½ cup **regular-strength chicken broth** or rich meat broth (page 16) and ½ cup **half-and-half** (light cream).

Return to heat and bring to a full rolling boil, stirring. Season to taste with **salt** and freshly grated (or ground) **nutmeg**. Use hot; or cover and chill, then reheat, stirring. Makes about 1 cup sauce.

Mornay sauce (*Sauce mornay*). Prepare **béchamel sauce** according to preceding directions, but omit nutmeg. Stir into simmering sauce 2 tablespoons shredded **Gruyère cheese** or Swiss cheese and 2 tablespoons grated **Parmesan cheese**.

Remove from heat and add **salt** and **cayenne** to taste. Use hot; or cover and chill, then reheat, stirring. Makes about 1 cup sauce.

MATTHEW NAYTHONS

Salad before, or with, the cheese

In the French household the salad follows the entrée, and its role is to refresh the palate for the fruit or sweet that ends the meal.

Cheese at the table, with or following the salad, is almost a ritual; crusty bread is a companion. It's a wholesome routine, one to consider also as the basis of a light lunch.

The most typical salad is plain crisp greens, perhaps several kinds mixed together, with a simple dressing.

Allow 1 cup salad greens and 1 to 2 tablespoons dressing for a serving; add salt to taste when you mix the salad.

Choose from the following, mixing and matching as you like.

"In Provence, the olive oil gives the flavor."

French salad choices, but any salad green is appropriate, including watercress, Belgian endive, escarole, romaine, dandelion greens. Greens with a bitter tang are often used with milder ones.

The dressings
(Les vinaigrettes)

The nature of a salad dressing in France depends upon the gleanings of the local harvest. In Provence, olives make the oil for most salads, while in Dordogne, plentiful walnuts are pressed and their oil is used. In Normandy, cream may take the place of oil, and cider vinegar, from the bounty of apples, can take the place of wine vinegar.

The dressings are best used within a day or two. Keep covered and in the refrigerator.

Housewife's dressing (*Vinaigrette bonne femme*). Blend 1 tablespoon *each* **Dijon mustard** and minced **shallots** or red onion, 3 tablespoons **wine vinegar**, and ½ cup **olive oil**. Makes ¾ cup.

Dordogne dressing (*Vinaigrette de Dordogne*). Blend 3 to 4 tablespoons **wine vinegar**, ½ cup **salad oil** or walnut oil, and 2 tablespoons coarsely chopped **walnuts**. Makes ¾ cup.

Bourbonnaise dressing (*Vinaigrette de Bourbon*). Blend 1 tablespoon *each* **Dijon mustard** and chopped **shallots** or red onion, 3 tablespoons **cider vinegar**, and ½ cup **salad oil**. Makes ¾ cup.

Crème fraîche dressing (*Vinaigrette à la crème*). Blend ½ cup **crème fraîche** (page 77), 1½ tablespoons **cider vinegar**, lemon juice, or wine vinegar, and 2 tablespoons minced **shallots** or chives. Makes ½ cup.

The greenery
(Les salades)

Wash salad greens well, drain or dry, then chill to crisp. Butter lettuce and chicory are very typical

The cheese
(Les fromages)

Imported from France are these cheeses that go well with salad. You can expect to find them in well-stocked cheese shops or (many of them) in large supermarkets in major metropolitan areas; if you have to make a special trip to purchase the cheeses, keep in mind that all the following, except the blue-veined cheeses and the double and triple cream cheeses, can be frozen up to 2 months. Freeze in serving-size portions. Do not refreeze.

Present cheeses from a tray or board; you can serve just one or several of the following (choose from different categories). Cut off pieces to eat with the salad.

Wine is served right along with this course; cheese is the perfect buffer for acid dressings that can detract from the palatability of the wine.

Semisoft cheeses: Port Salut, bonbel, Saint Paulin, tomme de Savoie, reblochon (trim rinds from individual portions if necessary).

Soft cheeses: Brie, Camembert, carré de l'est, Coulommiers, Livarot (rinds of these are edible); Pont l'Evêque (trim rind from individual portions).

Blue-veined cheeses: Roquefort, pipocrème, Bresse (no trimming required).

Goat cheeses (*chèvres*): Sainte-Maure, banon, pyramids, and others of different shapes (rind is edible unless coated with seasoning element—like ashes—or very hard).

Double and triple cream cheeses: boursault, boursin, caprice des Dieux, petit Suisse (no trimming required).

Processed cheeses: le beau pasteur, gourmandise, nec plus ultra.

"There is many a marriage for cheese and eggs."

Eggs and cheese

If a French cook were obliged to list the two most treasured foods, eggs would be one, and dairy products (an artful way to lump butter, milk, cream, and cheese) the other.

These ingredients are put to use in every conceivable way. All have made their appearance many times in the pages of this book, working hand-in-hand in many fine dishes. The making of crème fraîche, a tangy homemade sour cream used with much freedom in every chapter, is present—along with more ways to take advantage of its refreshing flavor.

The lighter, lower-calorie version of crème fraîche is white cheese (fromage blanc); you'll find directions for it here, and serving suggestions.

You can even use crème fraîche and white cheese as the first step toward making several easy but very elegant soft cheeses.

Some of the wizardry of which eggs are capable is deliciously demonstrated in custards—stirred and baked, savory and sweet, rich and light. Whipped eggs make airy meringues, soufflés, and omelet soufflés. (The emulsion sauces, pages 68 to 70, hail yet another talent of the egg.)

It's milk and eggs that make the thin and tender French pancakes (crêpes) that are perfectly tasty on their own and a dressy wrapping for almost any other food.

Cheese goes several steps beyond its own natural ready-to-eat state when mixed into salads, used in a simple ramekin, and added to omelets; it even converts custards into quiche. (For a discussion of cheeses to eat at the conclusion of a meal or with a salad, refer to page 71.)

Because of the exceptionally versatile nature of the principals of this chapter—eggs and cheese—the dishes here include first courses, entrées, salads, and desserts.

Eggs with crème fraîche
(Oeufs durs à la crème)

Serve as a first course or as part of a luncheon plate with cold meats and crudités (page 9).

Cut in half lengthwise 6 **hard-cooked eggs**. Arrange side by side in a serving dish and sprinkle with **salt**. Prepare **crème fraîche dressing** (page 71) and thin with **milk**, if necessary, to make a heavy pouring consistency. Spoon dressing over eggs. Sprinkle, if desired, with 2 tablespoons minced **chives** or parsley. Makes 3 to 6 first-course or side-dish servings.

Cheese ramekins
(Ramekins au fromage)

Essentially, this dish is nothing more than cheese melted on toast—but the toast is made extra crisp and the cheese is generous enough to become a sauce.

Select 6 to 8 small, shallow individual casseroles (½ to ¾-cup size). Cut a piece of **firm-textured white bread** to fit bottom of *each* dish. Place bread directly on oven rack. Bake at 200° for 45 minutes. Turn off heat and leave in closed oven for 1 hour.

Melt 8 to 10 tablespoons **butter** or margarine in a wide frying pan. Add bread and cook on low heat until golden brown on each side. Place a piece of the toast in each casserole.

Shred ¾ to 1 pound **cheese** (bonbel, fontina, provolone, teleme, jack, or other mild-flavor cheese that melts smoothly) and distribute evenly over toast, using all.

Cover and chill until ready to bake (until next day, if desired).

Bake, uncovered, in a 400° oven for 5 to 7 minutes or until cheese is bubbling. Accompany with crisp **radishes** and **green onions**. Makes 6 to 8 servings.

Cheese salad Androuët
(Salade de fromage Androuët)

Make this salad a first course or a lunch entrée, or turn it into a dinner salad by increasing the lettuce.

Blend ½ cup **sour cream** or crème fraîche (page 77) with 1 tablespoon *each* **Dijon mustard** and **lemon juice**, ¼ teaspoon *each* **basil leaves**, **tarragon leaves**, and **cumin seed**. (Cover and chill until next day, if desired.)

Cut ½ pound **Gruyère cheese** or Swiss, Edam, Jarlsberg, or samsoe cheese in matchstick-size slivers. Mix dressing with cheese and garnish with 2 to 4 **hard-cooked eggs**, cut in wedges. Makes 2 main-dish or 4 first-course servings.

To make into a dinner salad, combine **cheese mixture** with 6 tablespoons **milk** or half-and-half, then mix with 6 to 8 cups washed and crisped **butter lettuce** leaves, broken in small pieces. Makes 6 to 8 salads.

Poached eggs in red wine sauce
(Oeufs pochés des vignerons)

Hot poached eggs float in a steaming, robust wine sauce; both can be cooked ahead, then assembled.

Chop 1 medium-size **tomato** (peeled, if you like) and set aside. Finely chop 1 small **onion**. In a small pan cook onion in 1 tablespoon **butter** or margarine until soft, stirring on medium-high heat.

Add to onion the tomato and its juices, 1 cup **regular-strength chicken broth** or beef broth, or rich meat broth (page 16), 2 tablespoons **madeira**, 2 teaspoons **lemon juice**, ⅛ teaspoon **thyme leaves**, and ¹⁄₁₆ teaspoon **cayenne**. Bring sauce to a boil.

Blend smoothly 2 teaspoons *each* **cornstarch** and **water** and stir into boiling sauce. Cook, stirring, until slightly thickened. (If made ahead, cover and chill until next day; then reheat to continue.)

Divide sauce equally among 4 individual casseroles or small bowls (about ¾-cup size) and place in each 1 or 2 **hot poached eggs** (directions follow). Serve to eat with a spoon; accompany with **toast** and **butter**. Allow 1-egg portions as a first course, 2-egg portions as an entrée.

Poached eggs. First heat-set eggs (1 or 2 for a serving) in the shells by immersing in rapidly boiling water for 8 seconds.

Choose a pan large enough to accommodate, side by side, the number of eggs you want to cook. Fill pan with enough water to cover by 1 inch an egg out of shell.

Heat water until one or two bubbles break surface. Reduce heat, holding at a temperature that causes bubbles to form on pan bottom, with only an occasional one popping to top.

(Continued on next page)

Break each heat-set egg directly into water (do not crowd), holding as close to surface of water as possible.

Cook eggs until as set as you like—poke egg gently with a spoontip to check firmness. For soft yolks and firm whites, allow 3 to 5 minutes. Serve hot.

Or, to make ahead, lift eggs from hot water with a slotted spoon and immerse in ice water. Cover and chill until next day. To reheat, immerse cold egg in water that is just hot to touch and let stand 5 to 10 minutes. Drain and serve.

Crab omelet
(Omelette de crabe)

Make the sauce before you start this large omelet. Consider it for brunch, lunch, or supper.

Beat 6 **eggs** with 2 tablespoons **water** and ½ teaspoon **salt** just until blended.

In a 10 to 11-inch frying pan with rounded sides, melt 2 tablespoons **butter** or margarine over medium heat until sizzling. At once pour in eggs; as eggs begin to set, push from pan bottom to let uncooked egg flow into pan. Shake pan frequently to help keep eggs freely moving.

When eggs are set enough to no longer flow when pan is tipped, remove from heat and spread **crab sauce** (directions follow) over surface.

To fold, tip pan at about a 45° angle; with a spatula, fold about ⅓ of upper side of omelet down over filling.

Hold pan over a serving dish and shake so unfolded edge slips onto dish; then quickly flip pan on over so omelet folds onto itself into dish. Place a cluster of **watercress** alongside. Makes 3 servings.

Crab sauce. In a small pan melt 1 tablespoon **butter** or margarine and blend in 1 tablespoon **all-purpose flour**, ¼ cup **whipping cream**, and 1 tablespoon **madeira** or sherry. Bring to a boil, stirring. Mix in 1 cup **cooked crab** and a dash of **cayenne**. Heat through and keep warm until ready to use.

Tomato cream omelets
(Omelettes à la crème aux tomates)

Golden omelets sit in a hot lemon and cream base and are filled and decorated with a full-flavored tomato sauce.

Whirl smooth in a blender or food processor 1 medium-size **onion**, cut in chunks, and 3 tablespoons melted **butter** or margarine. Pour into a small pan and add 1 large can (12 oz.) **tomato paste**. Cook, stirring, on high heat until reduced to about ¾ cup; use hot. Or chill, covered, as long as 2 or 3 days; then reheat.

In a wide frying pan combine 1 tablespoon **lemon juice** and 1 cup **whipping cream**. Boil about 4 minutes on high heat until large shiny bubbles form. Pour cream evenly into 4 warm serving plates, using all; keep warm.

For 4 omelets break 8 **eggs** into a bowl and beat with 2 tablespoons **water** and ½ teaspoon **salt** just until blended.

To cook *each* omelet, melt 2 tablespoons **butter** or margarine in a 6 or 7-inch omelet pan over high heat. When sizzling, add ¼ of the eggs (about ⅓ cup); push eggs from pan bottom as they set, allowing uncooked portion to flow down into pan. Shake pan frequently to keep eggs freely moving.

When eggs are as set as you like, spoon 2 tablespoons tomato sauce down center.

To fold, tilt pan at about a 45° angle and, with a spatula or fork, fold about ⅓ of upper side of omelet down over filling. Hold pan over dish with cream and shake so unfolded edge slips out onto dish; then quickly flip pan on over so omelet folds onto itself into dish. Keep warm until all omelets are cooked.

Spoon remaining tomato sauce equally in dollops onto omelets. Garnish with **parsley** or watercress sprigs. Makes 4 servings.

Herb omelet
(Omelette aux fines herbes)

A combination of herbs makes for new omelet flavors. Top with Parmesan cheese if you like.

Finely chop ¼ cup **chives** or green onion (including some tops) and mix with 1 small clove **garlic**, minced or pressed, and ¼ teaspoon *each* crumbled **tarragon leaves**, **basil leaves**, and **thyme leaves**.

Follow omelet directions in tomato cream omelets (preceding), omitting cream sauce and tomato sauce. Use 9 eggs instead of 8 and make 3 omelets instead of 4, filling each with ⅓ of chive mixture. If desired, also sprinkle 1 tablespoon shredded **Parmesan cheese** over each omelet before folding. Makes 3 servings.

Eggs with watercress mayonnaise
(Oeufs durs à la mayonnaise au cresson)

Simple, but fresh in flavors. Have hard-cooked eggs shelled and sauce made; then put this dish together on a moment's notice.

Shell 6 to 8 **hard-cooked eggs**. Place 1 egg in each individual serving dish. Pour evenly over eggs 1 recipe's worth **watercress mayonnaise** (page 69), using all. Garnish with **watercress** sprigs. Makes 6 to 8 first-course servings.

VELVETY GREEN CASCADE of watercress mayonnaise coats hard-cooked eggs for speedy first course; additional watercress leaves are nippy-tasting garnish.

Piperade

(Pipérade à la basquaise)

Choose an attractive frying pan for making this colorful Basque-style flat omelet, because you serve from the cooking utensil.

Cook bacon, vegetables, then eggs in sequence in the same pan.

Cut 2 slices **bacon** in small pieces. Place in a 10 to 11-inch frying pan over medium-low heat and cook until bacon is crisp and brown. With a slotted spoon, lift meat from drippings and set aside.

To pan add 1 small **green pepper**, seeded and cut in thin slivers; cook, stirring, on medium heat until limp but still bright green.

Add to pan 1 small **tomato**, peeled, seeded and diced; 1 cup (about ¼ lb.) coarsely chopped **cooked ham**; and 2 tablespoons chopped **parsley**. Cook, stirring gently, until heated. With slotted spoon, lift out vegetables and set aside; keep warm.

Beat 8 **eggs** with 2 tablespoons **water** and ½ teaspoon **salt** just until blended. Pour into frying pan and cook over low heat. Push eggs from pan bottom as they cook, letting liquid egg flow down to heat. When eggs are almost as set as you like, distribute vegetables and ham over surface and continue cooking, gently shaking pan, until eggs are set. Sprinkle with bacon and serve from pan. Makes 3 to 4 servings.

Country omelet
(Omelette brayaude)

"No quicker meal."

The toppings of this open-faced omelet are contrasts in flavors and textures: crunchy bacon, tender bits of cooked potato and onion, cheese in both chewy chunks and lacy shreds, cool sour cream, and crisp sautéed walnuts.

The longest cooking steps can be completed ahead.

In a 10 or 11-inch frying pan, cook 4 slices **bacon** over medium-low heat until crisp and brown. Lift out bacon, break in pieces, and set aside.

To drippings add about 24 **walnut halves**. Cook, stirring gently, over medium heat for 1 to 2 minutes or until lightly toasted; lift out nuts and set aside.

Discard all but 4 tablespoons drippings from pan. Peel and cut in ⅛-inch dice enough **new potato** to make ½ cup; also cut 1 small **onion** in ⅛-inch dice. Add potato and onion to pan and cook over medium-low heat for about 20 minutes, until potato is soft to bite but only slightly browned. Pour from pan and keep warm (as long as 1 hour) or reheat.

To cook omelet, clean frying pan, then add 3 tablespoons **butter** or margarine and melt over medium-low heat. Beat 6 to 8 **eggs** with ¼ teaspoon **salt** just until blended. Pour eggs into butter; push eggs from pan bottom as they set, letting liquid egg flow down into pan. When eggs are almost set (still a little liquid-looking) sprinkle evenly with warm potato and onion, ½ cup diced (about ⅛-inch pieces) **Swiss cheese**, ¼ cup shredded **Swiss cheese**, and 2 tablespoons minced **parsley**.

Remove from heat and mound ½ cup **crème fraîche** (right) or sour cream in center and garnish with toasted walnuts.

Cut in wedges and serve with a wide spatula. Makes 4 to 6 servings.

Cream hearts
(Coeurs à la crème)

Use heart-shaped molds of ceramic (with drainage holes, page 7) or natural-finish baskets to give this simple dessert its classic form.

Prepare **white cheese** according to directions (right). Line a 2-cup heart-shaped mold or 4 smaller molds (½-cup size) with 4 layers washed cheesecloth, letting cloth drape over sides of mold. (Or you can use plain molds of same volume.)

Spoon white cheese into mold or molds and loosely fold cloth ends over cheese. Set molds on a rack (about ½ inch high) in a rimmed pan. Wrap entire unit in clear plastic film (to prevent contamination of cheese by other flavors) and place in refrigerator for at least 24 hours or as long as 48.

To serve, pull cloth back from cheese and turn cheese out onto a plate.

Serve large mold to cut in portions for 4. Serve small molds individually.

Sprinkle with **sugar** (plain or vanilla) and accompany with **sweet biscuits**—such as petit beurre—and **fresh fruits**—such as strawberries, raspberries, or cherries. Makes 4 servings.

Garlic and herb cheese
(Fromage à l'ail et aux fines herbes)

This cheese is much like boursin and can be served in the same manner.

Peel 4 cloves **garlic**, tie loosely in washed cheesecloth, and crush lightly with back of spoon.

Start **crème fraîche** as directed (right), using 2 cups **whipping cream**; add garlic bag along with **buttermilk** (do not use sour cream; it forms a softer cheese).

When cream has chilled at least 24 hours, lift out garlic bag, squeezing as much juice as possible into cream.

Line a colander with a muslin cloth; set in sink and pour in cream. Let drain about 1 hour. Set colander in a rimmed pan and package airtight; chill at least 12 hours or until next day.

Scoop cheese into a bowl and blend in ¼ teaspoon **salt** (or to taste), ¼ teaspoon **basil leaves**, and ⅛ teaspoon *each* **tarragon leaves**, **thyme leaves**, **rosemary leaves**, and **rubbed sage**.

Line a 1 to 2-cup ceramic mold (with drainage holes) or natural-finish basket with 4 layers washed cheesecloth. Spoon cheese into cloth, then fold cloth over cheese. Place on a rack in a small pan, package airtight, and chill at least 12 hours or as long as 5 days. Fold back cloth and unmold cheese to serve. Makes 1 cheese about 1-cup size (you can double recipe to make 2 cheeses).

Cheese quiches or cheese tarts

(Quiches au fromage ou tartes de fromage)

You can start a meal with these small tarts, or eat them as a snack. The tarts are also well liked for picnicking.

Measure **pastry dough** (recipe follows) according to pan size and press evenly over bottom of pan and up sides flush with rim. Allow about 2 tablespoons dough to line a 1 by 3-inch tart pan; use 2½ tablespoons dough for a 1 by 4-inch pan. Set pans on a baking sheet. To each pan add 2 tablespoons shredded **Swiss cheese** or Gruyère cheese.

Beat 2 **eggs**. Blend with 1½ cups **half-and-half** (light cream) and a dash of **pepper**. Pour liquid evenly into pastry shells (don't let it overflow or pastry will stick).

Set baking sheet on lowest rack in a 350° oven. Bake for 35 to 40 minutes or until filling puffs (it settles when cooled) and tops are lightly browned.

Let quiches cool about 10 minutes; then, protecting your hand, tip them out of pans into your hand and place, filling side up, on a rack to cool further. Or you can serve them hot. (If you make quiches a day ahead, cover and chill. Serve at room temperature or reheat: place side by side on a baking sheet in a 350° oven for 10 minutes.)

Hot or cooled, quiches can be served on a plate to eat with a fork. Cooled, they are good eaten out of hand, too. Makes about 8 quiches 4-inch size, 10 quiches 3-inch size.

Pastry dough. In a bowl, combine 1½ cups unsifted **all-purpose flour** and ¼ teaspoon **salt**. Add 10 tablespoons (¼ lb. plus 2 tablespoons) **butter** or margarine, cut into chunks, and mix to coat with flour.

With fingers or a pastry blender, rub or cut butter into flour until you have fine particles. Add 1 **egg** and stir with a fork until dough holds together. Shape dough into a ball (if made ahead, cover and chill; use at room temperature). Makes 1½ cups.

White cheese with crème fraîche

(Fromage blanc à la crème fraîche)

Fresh fruit is often served with these dairy foods, sharing the same plate.

Crème fraîche and fromage blanc: household staples

Crème fraîche can be considered a staple in French cookery; it has the richness of our whipping cream, but the consistency and tang of sour cream. Yet it doesn't curdle or separate when heated. Mild flavor whipping cream can be used as an alternate.

White cheese is prepared the same way as crème fraîche, but is made with milk; because the butterfat content is lower, it cannot be used in cooking like crème fraîche. White cheese is more tart in flavor than crème fraîche and softer in texture, but it can be used as a topping for soups and fruits and in other similar ways.

To start both crème fraîche and white cheese, you warm the liquid, than add buttermilk as a starter, which causes the liquid to clot. Time does the work.

Crème fraîche

(Crème fraîche)

For each 1 cup **whipping cream**, warmed to 90° to 100°, add 1 tablespoon **buttermilk** or sour cream (select a brand for its flavor; there is a range in tastes), blending well. Cover and let stand at room temperature (68° to 72°—or put in a yogurt maker) for 12 to 16 hours or until it begins to thicken.

Chill at least 24 hours before using to allow acid flavor to develop and cream to thicken further; cream should then be of almost spreadable consistency. Store in refrigerator up to 2 weeks or as long as taste is tangy but fresh. Makes 1 cup.

White cheese

(Fromage blanc)

Follow directions for crème fraîche (preceding), using 4 cups **whole milk** instead of whipping cream, and ¼ cup **buttermilk** (do not use sour cream).

The finished product will have a yogurtlike consistency. Pour into a cloth-lined colander and let drain for 2 to 3 hours.

Scoop white cheese into a covered container and chill until ready to use or as long as a week.

Serve white cheese as you would sour cream or crème fraîche when heat is not used. Makes about 2 cups.

Spoon **white cheese** (above) onto plate (allowing ⅓ to ½ cup for a portion) and spoon **crème fraîche** (above) on top (2 to 3 tablespoons for a portion). Sprinkle with **sugar**.

Quiche Lorraine
(Quiche Lorraine)

The addition of cooked bacon to a quiche is a touch sometimes credited to the cooks of Lorraine, in eastern France.

Make **pastry dough** as directed for cheese quiches (page 77). Roll out on a well-floured board and fit into a 10-inch pie pan or tart dish or pan. Make dough flush with top rim, folding excess dough against pan sides and pressing firmly in place. (Dough tears easily, but does not toughen; pinch tears together to rejoin.)

Coarsely chop 10 slices **cooked bacon** and scatter in pastry shell; sprinkle with 1¼ cups diced (¼-inch cubes) **Swiss cheese** or Gruyère cheese (about ½ lb.). Beat 4 **eggs** to blend with 1¼ cups **whipping cream** or half-and-half (light cream) and ½ cup **milk**. Pour into pastry. Grate a little **nutmeg** over filling.

Place on lowest rack in a 350° oven and bake for about 55 minutes or until filling is slightly puffed and lightly browned on top. Let stand at least 10 minutes before cutting in wedges; quiche may be served hot, warm, at room temperature, or cold. Makes 8 to 10 first-course servings or 6 main-dish servings.

Snow eggs or floating islands
(Oeufs à la neige)

Classically there is a distinction between snow eggs and floating islands, but in practice the names are used interchangeably. They describe cooked soft meringues served in a custard sauce, with a crackling, crunchy topping of caramel.

Snow eggs, according to tradition, are snowy white, oval-shaped, poached meringues; floating islands are dropped puffs of meringue—each with a multitude of little peaks—that are baked and poached at the same time, so the peaks are tinged with brown. Because the latter procedure is less time-consuming, it is generally preferred, as the dessert is a great favorite in the homes and restaurants of France.

Separate 4 **eggs**; set whites aside. Place yolks in top of a double broiler and add 2 more **eggs** (both whites and yolks), ⅓ cup **vanilla sugar** (or use plain sugar and 1½ teaspoons vanilla); mix thoroughly.

OEUFS À LA NEIGE is a showy dessert of simple ingredients—eggs, cream, and sugar. Amber ribbons of melted sugar meander crisply over tender meringue puffs and melt in caramel streaks through chilled custard base.

Heat to scalding 3 cups **half-and-half** (light cream) and stir into eggs. With top of double boiler nestled in gently **simmering water**, cook, stirring constantly, until custard coats a metal spoon in a velvety smooth layer; cooking time varies with rate of heat, but expect it to take 10 to 15 minutes for custard to thicken.

At once, set double boiler top with custard into **ice water** to stop the cooking; stir frequently until cool. Stir in 2 tablespoons **Grand Marnier**. Pour custard into a 2 to 3-quart serving bowl; cover and chill (until next day, if you like).

With an electric mixer, whip reserved egg whites and ¼ teaspoon **cream of tartar** until foamy. Whipping at high speed, gradually add ⅔ cup **sugar** (plain or vanilla) and beat until peaks form which curl slightly when beater is withdrawn.

Place a large shallow pan (about size of a broiler pan) in a 400° oven and pour about 1 inch **boiling water** into pan.

From a spoon, drop large scoops (make 6 to 8 total) of meringue into water; do not overlap. Bake, uncovered, for 5 to 8 minutes or until meringues are golden.

Quickly remove from oven and lift meringues from water with a slotted spoon, draining well. You can mound meringues onto chilled custard; or you can set them side by side in a rimmed pan and chill, covered, without touching, until next day—then mound them onto chilled custard.

As long as 4 hours before time to serve, you can complete dessert. Place ¼ cup **sugar** in a small frying pan. Place on medium heat to melt sugar; shake pan to mix sugar as it begins to liquefy and caramelize. When liquid (do not let scorch) pour *at once* onto meringue stack, letting caramel drizzle down on all sides (if you use a glass bowl, the showiest container for this dessert, caramel should cause no problem if it flows from meringues up against glass). Serve; or keep cold, covered.

Crack through caramel with serving spoon and place a meringue and about ½ cup sauce in each individual bowl. Makes 6 to 8 servings.

To make 12 to 16 servings, double the preceding recipe. (This is a most effective dish for a large party, and it can be made ahead.) Custard will take a few minutes longer to cook. Use a 3 to 4-quart serving bowl.

Custard sauce
(Crème anglaise)

Soft custard is often spooned onto ice cream or fruit—or both together. Sweetened whipped cream may be an additional topping.

This sauce also can be spooned onto servings of savarin (page 87) or uniced cakes.

(Continued on next page)

If you keep a bowl of the custard in the refrigerator, any number of other uses will soon suggest themselves.

Make **custard** as directed for **snow eggs** (page 79), but use 4 whole **eggs** instead of 4 yolks with 2 whole eggs, and reduce **half-and-half** to 2 cups (or use 2 cups milk). Flavor to taste, if desired, with **liqueur** such as Grand Marnier, kirsch, framboise, cointreau (or other orange-flavored liqueur), rum, brandy, madeira.

You can serve custard as a dessert in bowls (½ to ⅔ cup for a portion) or as a sauce for other foods. Chill, covered; sauce can be kept 3 or 4 days. Makes about 2½ cups.

Chantilly custard

(Crème anglaise à la Chantilly)

When whipped cream is folded into custard, it makes a fluffy-textured sauce of the same versatility.

Beat 1 cup **whipping cream** until soft peaks form when mixer is lifted. Fold in 1 recipe's worth **custard sauce** (preceding). If refrigerated, stir before using; can be kept 3 or 4 days. Makes about 4 cups.

Petite vanilla custards

(Pots de crème à la vanille)

Rich and luxuriantly smooth custard baked in tiny individual cups makes pots de crème. The cups made especially for this dish (page 7) are usually about ½-cup capacity and come with lids; however, other small containers such as oriental teacups or stoneware jars of the same size can be used as alternatives, and foil can cap them during baking. Many flavor variations are possible.

Split a 3-inch section of **vanilla bean** lengthwise. Combine with 2 cups **half-and-half** (light cream) and ½ cup **sugar**. Heat to scalding, stirring. Cover and let stand until cooled (about 30 minutes). Remove vanilla bean.

Again, heat cream to scalding, stirring. With a fork, gradually blend into 6 slightly beaten **egg yolks**. Pour mixture through a fine wire strainer into 6 individual cups (about ½-cup size), dividing equally. Cover cups with lids or foil and set in a rimmed baking pan.

Place in a 350° oven and at once pour in enough **boiling water** to make 1-inch depth. Bake for about 25 minutes or until center of custard jiggles just slightly when a cup is shaken. Lift from hot water and remove lids; let cool to room temperature.

Cover again and chill until time to serve (as long as 2 days). Makes 6 servings.

For a simpler vanilla custard, omit vanilla bean and first scalding step; add 1 teaspoon **vanilla** to egg and cream mixture (preceding).

For a liqueur-flavored custard, instead of the vanilla (immediately preceding), use 2 to 3 tablespoons (or to taste) **cointreau**, crème de cacao (light or dark), Grand Marnier, Strega, or other liqueur of your choice.

Petite coffee custards

(Pots de crème au café)

First you infuse the cream with coffee, then use the cream for the custard.

Follow directions for **petite vanilla custards** (preceding), but omit vanilla bean. Use instead 3 tablespoons **ground coffee**. Pour cream through a muslin cloth and discard coffee grounds. Also add 1 tablespoon **coffee-flavored liqueur** such as Kahlúa.

"I use lots of cream because I come from Normandy."

Caramel custard

(Crème renversée au caramel)

Caramelized sugar coats the bottoms of the cups in which the custard bakes, creating a sauce.

In a small frying pan over medium heat, melt ⅓ cup **sugar**, shaking pan to mix sugar as it begins to liquefy and caramelize. When liquid (do not let scorch), pour at once, equally, into 4 small, deep baking dishes (*each* at least ⅔-cup size).

In a bowl, beat until blended, but not frothy, 4 **eggs**, ¼ cup **sugar**, and ½ teaspoon **vanilla**. Bring 2 cups **milk** to scalding and stir into eggs. Pour an equal portion into each baking dish.

Set dishes in a rimmed pan and place in a 350°

oven; at once pour **boiling water** into pan to a depth of about 1 inch.

Bake for about 25 minutes or until center of custard jiggles only slightly when a dish is shaken gently. Lift from water at once and let cool; serve at room temperature or cover and chill as long as 2 days.

Run a knife between custard and dish, then invert onto individual serving plates. Makes 4 servings.

Butter cream crêpes with jam

(Crêpes à la crème au beurre avec confiture)

Flame these simple crêpes at the table for a bit of drama. Or you can skip the flaming altogether.

Combine ¼ cup room-temperature **butter** or margarine and 1 cup unsifted **powdered sugar** and beat until smoothly blended; stir in 2 tablespoons **rum** or kirsch. Spread butter cream evenly over one side of each of 16 **French pancakes** (at right).

Then drizzle about 2 teaspoons **jam** down center of each crêpe—use tart berry jam with rum-flavored butter cream; apricot or cherry jam with kirsch-flavored butter cream. Roll each crêpe around jam to form a slender cylinder.

Place rolls, side by side and seam side down, in a shallow 2 to 2½-quart baking pan. Cover and chill until ready to heat.

Bake, covered, in a 400° oven for 15 to 20 minutes or until crêpes in center of pan are warmed.

To serve, set ¼ cup warmed **rum** or kirsch aflame and pour over crêpes (*not beneath an exhaust fan or flammable items*); with a long-handled spoon, ladle juices in pan over crêpes continuously (to prevent edges from singeing) until flame dies. Serve crêpes with **sweetened whipped cream**, if desired. Makes 5 to 8 servings.

Crêpes mylene

(Crêpes mylene)

An airy-textured cream fills these oven-heated crêpes.

In a small pan stir together 3 tablespoons **cornstarch** and ¼ cup **sugar** (plain or vanilla). Gradually stir in 1 cup **half-and-half** (light cream). On medium heat, bring to a vigorous boil, stirring; sauce is very thick. Remove from heat and beat in 2 eggs, 1 at a time. Cook on low heat, stirring, for 3 minutes; do not boil. Add 1 teaspoon **vanilla**. Cover and chill (as long as next day), stirring once or twice. Dot a shallow 3-quart casserole with 2 tablespoons **butter** or margarine; set aside.

With an electric mixer at high speed, beat 2 **egg whites** and ⅛ teaspoon **cream of tartar** until foamy, then add gradually ¼ cup **sugar**; beat until stiff peaks hold when beater is lifted.

Stir a spoonful of meringue into chilled cream, then fold cream and balance of meringue together.

Lay out side by side 12 **French pancakes** (following). Spoon an equal portion of cream mixture (about ¼ cup) down center of each, using all the cream. Fold sides of crêpe up and over filling.

Handling gently, place crêpes seam side down and side by side in casserole. (Cover and chill as long as 2 hours, if you wish.)

Bake, covered, in a 400° oven for 10 minutes (15 if chilled).

Remove from oven. Set aflame 6 tablespoons warmed **Grand Marnier** and pour over crêpes (at table, if desired; *not beneath an exhaust fan or flammable items*); shake casserole until flame dies. Makes 6 servings of 2 crêpes each.

Basic crêpes

Crêpes enjoy a remarkable range of presentation in France. They are eaten as snacks and incorporated into any meal, even the most elegant.

French pancakes

(Crêpes)

With a wire whip (or in a blender or food processor) blend 3 **eggs** and ⅔ cup unsifted **all-purpose flour**. Gradually add 1 cup **milk**, mixing until smooth.

Place a 6 to 7-inch crêpe pan (page 7) or other flat-bottomed frying pan of this size on medium heat. When pan is hot, add ¼ teaspoon **butter** or margarine and swirl to coat surface. At once pour in about 1½ tablespoons batter, tilting pan so batter flows quickly over entire flat surface. If heat is correct and pan hot enough, crêpe sets at once, forming tiny bubbles (don't worry if there are a few little holes); if pan is too cool, batter makes a smooth layer. Cook crêpe until edge is lightly browned and surface looks dry.

Because this crêpe tears easily, use this technique for turning: Run a wide spatula around edge to loosen. Lay spatula on top of crêpe and invert pan, turning crêpe out onto spatula. Then guide crêpe, uncooked surface down, back into pan and brown lightly. Turn crêpe out of pan onto a plate.

Repeat this procedure to make each crêpe; stir batter occasionally and stack crêpes one atop another. If you do not use them within a few hours, package airtight when cool and refrigerate as long as a week; or freeze for longer storage. Allow crêpes to come to room temperature before separating, as they tear if cold.

To reheat crêpes, if you just want to eat them with **butter** and **jam**, stack crêpes (as many as 1 recipe's worth) and seal in foil. Place in a 350° oven for 10 to 15 minutes. Makes about 16 crêpes.

Citrus crêpes

(Crêpes Suzette)

When you assemble crêpes Suzette at the table, borrow some of the showmanship techniques that restaurateurs employ effectively—such as squeezing the orange and lemon juice directly into the chafing dish.

Fold 12 to 16 **French pancakes** (page 81) in half.

In a wide frying pan or chafing dish over medium-high heat (or large alcohol flame) melt ¼ cup **butter** or margarine and add 6 tablespoons **sugar**. Cook, stirring, until bubbling vigorously (do not brown butter).

Add 1½ teaspoons grated **orange peel**, ½ teaspoon grated **lemon peel**, ⅓ cup **orange juice** (or, at table, squeeze juice by hand from half a large, juicy orange), and 2 teaspoons **lemon juice** (or, at table, squeeze about this much juice from half a lemon) and bring sauce to a full rolling boil. Add crêpes, one at a time, to sauce, and as each is moistened by sauce, fold the half to make a triangle.

When all crêpes are heated, set aflame ¼ cup warmed **cointreau** (or other orange-flavored liqueur, including Grand Marnier) and pour over crêpes (*not beneath an exhaust fan or flammable items*). Shake pan until flame dies. Let simmer a few minutes, then spoon crêpes and sauce onto serving dishes. Allow 2 or 3 for a serving, and accompany, if you like, with **orange slices**. Makes 5 to 8 servings.

Grand Marnier soufflé

(Soufflé au Grand Marnier)

Soufflés are reputed to have a last-minute nature that intimidates many cooks. But you can complete the most time-consuming step—the sauce—hours ahead, then fold in the whipped egg whites just before baking.

Butter and dust with **sugar** a 1½-quart soufflé dish. Cut a sheet of foil that is 4 inches longer than circumference of soufflé dish. Fold lengthwise in thirds (for strength), then form a collar by wrapping around outside of dish so at least 2 inches of foil extend above dish rim; fold ends over and over until snug against dish, or secure with masking tape. Butter the collar inside.

Melt ¼ cup **butter** or margarine in a small pan. Add ¼ cup unsifted **all-purpose flour** and ½ cup **sugar**. Cook, stirring, until bubbling.

Remove from heat and gradually blend in 1 cup **milk** or half-and-half (light cream). Add ½ teaspoon grated **orange peel**, and ¼ teaspoon grated **lemon peel**.

Stirring, bring to a vigorous boil on high heat. Remove from heat. (At this point you can cover and chill sauce until next day; reheat to continue.)

Stir in ¼ cup **Grand Marnier** (or cointreau or curaçao) and 6 **egg yolks**.

With an electric mixer, whip at high speed 6 **egg whites** with ¼ teaspoon **cream of tartar** until whites hold very soft peaks when beater is lifted. Continue at high speed and gradually add ¼ cup **sugar**, beating until short, distinct peaks form when beater is lifted. Stir about ⅓ of whites into sauce, then gently fold sauce into remaining whites.

Pour soufflé mixture into prepared dish. Bake, uncovered, on low rack in a 375° oven for 35 to 40 minutes for a soufflé with a saucy center. After 25 minutes, with soufflé in oven, quickly open seam of foil collar and slip collar off so portion of soufflé above dish will brown lightly.

Spoon out and serve at once with **sweetened whipped cream** (use 1 cup whipping cream), flavored to taste with **Grand Marnier**, if desired. Makes 6 servings.

Lemon omelet soufflé

(Omelette soufflée au citron)

Thicker, creamier, and moister than a regular soufflé, omelet soufflés are an airy combination of whipped egg whites and whipped egg yolks sweetened, flavored, folded together, and baked.

Omelet soufflés are quick to make, and they bake quickly; put one together when the salad or cheese is being served.

Separate 6 **eggs**, placing yolks in one mixing bowl, whites in another.

Whip whites at high speed with an electric mixer until short, stiff peaks form when beater is lifted; then gradually, mixing at high speed, beat in ¼ cup **sugar** until whites hold stiff peaks when beater is lifted.

With same beater at high speed, whip egg yolks with another ¼ cup **sugar** and ½ teaspoon grated **lemon peel** until very thick and lighter in color. Fold yolks thoroughly into whites.

Combine 3 tablespoons *each* **butter** or margarine, **sugar**, and **lemon juice**, and ¼ teaspoon grated **lemon peel** in a 10-inch ovenproof frying pan and cook, stirring, over high heat until bubbling vigorously. At once remove from heat and spoon (do not mix) egg mixture into frying pan in large dollops.

Bake in a 350° oven for 15 to 20 minutes or until omelet soufflé is set around edge, moist and slightly creamy in center, and a golden brown.

Spoon into butter sauce when you ladle out portions of soufflé. Top each serving with **sweetened whipped cream** (about 1 cup whipping cream). Makes 6 to 8 servings.

Breads and desserts

"Feast the eye before the stomach."

When a Frenchman wants his bread, he goes to the boulangerie (bakery); when a sweet is in order, it often means a trip to the pâtisserie (pastry shop).

It comes as a surprise to most first-time visitors to France that buying many of these foods is more commonplace than preparing them. The practice is actually a holdover from times when bakers had the best ovens in town, and the pâtisserie had not only an oven, but a freezer as well. True convenience, we must admit, is to just run around the corner to pick up the finished first-class product—and the logic of the French to cling to such "old-fashioned" ways is a wisdom to admire.

In this chapter you get a cross sampling of professional artistry and domestic favorites—because there are a few recipes in this chapter dear to home cooks, too; see the preceding chapter for more of them.

When you duplicate such time-consuming and worthy efforts as baguettes, brioches, or croissants, it is practical to capitalize on the fact that the results freeze beautifully; you can keep a supply of these fine breads on hand.

By the same token, various elements of all the remaining desserts in this chapter can be frozen; this means your freezer can bring you much of the same convenience as a shop around the corner.

If the meal is simple, you can end with just fruit in its natural state, to eat rather ceremoniously with knife and fork. Perhaps the habit of fruit with each meal is one clue as to how the sauce-loving French maintain trim waistlines.

On more auspicious occasions a dessert will come before the fruit; if the sweet is basically fruit, such as a tart or berries with cream, additional fruit will likely be omitted.

The final sweet adieu is usually small cups of strong coffee, served away from the dining table.

Baguettes

(Baguettes)

These are the long, skinny, crusty loaves seen protruding from the shopping baskets of French housewives, strapped onto bicycles, or carried under the arms of French workmen.

You can't quite fit the typical 2-foot-long baguette into a conventional-size oven, but you can probably bake a loaf that's at least 18 inches long—measure the diagonal dimension of your oven.

This recipe makes a loaf with the shiny, crisp crust and chewy texture much like genuine French bread. Baguettes are best baked and eaten on the same day, ideally still warm from the oven. If you can't use all three loaves the first day, freeze extras and reheat to crisp before serving.

You need a pan that measures at least 18 inches diagonally and that will fit in your oven with at least 1 inch of free space between pan and oven walls on all four sides. (Or you can overlap two smaller rimless baking sheets to make this dimension; lay a sheet of foil on top to make a smooth surface.)

Soften 1 package **active dry yeast** in ¼ cup **warm water** (about 110°). Add 1½ tablespoons **sugar**, 2 teaspoons **salt**, 1¾ cup **warm water** (about 110°), and 5½ cups unsifted **all-purpose flour**. Mix with a heavy spoon until flour is moistened and dough clings together.

Turn dough onto a board coated with ½ cup unsifted **all-purpose flour** and knead for 10 to 15 minutes or until dough is smooth and feels velvety. Add more flour to board if needed to prevent sticking.

Place dough in a greased bowl; turn dough over to grease top. Cover bowl with clear plastic film and let stand in a warm place until dough rises almost double (1 to 1½ hours). Punch down dough, then turn out onto a lightly floured board and divide into 3 equal pieces.

If you have only one oven, wrap 2 pieces of dough in clear plastic film and refrigerate.

On a lightly floured board, form one piece of dough into a smooth log by gently kneading and rolling dough back and forth until it is 10 to 12 inches long. For a smooth, well-shaped loaf, press a trench lengthwise down center of dough; then fold dough in half lengthwise along trench. With a gentle kneading motion, seal along edge by pressing against fold with heel of your hand, rolling and pushing sealed edge underneath.

With palms of your hands on center of loaf, begin rolling it back and forth rapidly, gently pulling from center to ends as you slide your hands toward ends until loaf is about 18 to 20 inches long (length will depend on oven size).

Place loaf diagonally across a large greased baking sheet (see notes on pan size in recipe introduction); cover lightly with clear plastic film. Let rise in a warm place for about 15 to 20 minutes or until it is puffy-looking but not doubled in size.

Put 1 teaspoon **cornstarch** in a small pan. Smoothly blend in ⅔ cup **water**. Bring to boiling, stirring; cool slightly. Uncover loaf and brush with cornstarch mixture, making sure to moisten sides of loaf down to baking sheet.

With a sharp knife or razor blade, cut slanting, ½-inch-deep slashes at 2-inch intervals down length of loaf.

Bake in a 375° oven for 15 minutes; then evenly brush loaf again with cornstarch mixture. Bake 15 minutes longer and brush with cornstarch mixture. Bake about 10 minutes longer or until loaf is golden brown and makes a hollow sound when tapped (about 35 to 40 minutes total). Cool on wire rack.

When you put first loaf in oven to bake, remove second piece of dough from refrigerator and shape like first loaf; place second loaf on a piece of foil to rise. It will take about 30 minutes to rise until puffy-looking (third loaf will take slightly longer). Bake as directed.

As you put second loaf in to bake, shape third piece of dough, let rise, and then bake as directed.

For maximum flavor and freshness, serve bread same day it is baked; or cool completely, wrap airtight, and freeze. Bread will regain its crispness when reheated. To reheat, place thawed loaves directly on rack of a 350° oven for 15 to 20 minutes. Makes 3 long loaves.

Brioche dough

(Pâte à brioche)

Egg-and-butter-rich brioche dough is used to shape many kinds of brioche breads. Most familiar are the individual rolls, petites brioches; this top-knotted shape on a grander scale is called "brioche à tête," or brioche with a head.

The same dough (or it might be flavored additionally) can be used for making ring loaves or crowns or tall cylindrical loaves, and it deliciously encases other foods such as salmon in brioche (page 27), and so on, depending on local traditions and the whim of the cook.

But in common they share deep golden crusts, light golden interiors, a feathery, springy texture, and wonderful fragrance and flavor.

Part of the character of this bread comes from an overnight proofing (or rising) in the refrigerator—so plan to start at least a day before serving. These breads also freeze well.

In a large mixing bowl combine ½ cup **warm**

water (about 110°) and 1 package **active dry yeast**; let stand about 5 minutes to soften. Stir in 2 teaspoons **sugar**, 1¼ teaspoons **salt**, and 3 **eggs**. Cut ½ cup (¼ lb.) room-temperature **butter** or margarine in small pieces and add to liquid along with 3⅓ cups unsifted **all-purpose flour**.

If you have a dough hook, mix until dough pulls cleanly from bowl sides.

If mixing by hand, stir until flour is evenly moistened and dough holds together; then shape in a ball and place on a floured board. Knead until smooth and velvety (takes about 5 minutes). Add more flour to board if needed to prevent sticking. Rinse and grease mixing bowl, add dough, and turn over once to grease top. Cover with clear plastic film and let rise in a warm place until doubled in volume (takes at least 1 hour, but may take 2).

Knead dough on a lightly floured board to expel air (or mix with dough hook). Return to greased bowl, cover with clear plastic film, and refrigerate 12 to 24 hours.

Stir, or knead on floured board to expel air. Shape dough and bake according to directions that follow.

Individual brioches

(Petites brioches)

Breakfast in France means a warm petite brioche and/or croissant, a big chunk of sweet butter, some good jam, and steaming cups of café au lait (coffee with hot milk).

But consider these attractive rolls for other meals as well.

Divide 1 recipe's worth **brioche dough** (preceding) in 24 equal pieces. Dough is easiest to handle if kept cool, so shape a few brioches at a time, keeping remaining pieces separated, covered, and refrigerated until ready to use.

To shape *each* brioche, pinch off about ⅙ of each portion and set aside. Shape larger section into a smooth ball by pulling surface of dough to underside of ball; this is very important if you want to achieve a good-looking brioche.

Set ball, smooth side up, in a well-buttered 3 to 4-inch petite brioche pan (page 7), 3 to 4-inch fluted tart pan, or 3-inch muffin cup. Press dough down to fill pan bottom evenly.

Shape small piece of dough into a teardrop shape that is smooth on top.

With your finger, poke a hole in center of brioche dough in pan and insert pointed end of small piece in hole, settling securely (otherwise, topknot will pop off at an angle while baking). Repeat until all brioches are shaped. (If you work quickly you can leave pans at room temperature when

filled; otherwise, return filled pans, lightly covered, to refrigerator.)

Cover filled pans lightly with clear plastic film and let stand in a warm place until about doubled in size (takes 1 to 2 hours). Remove cover.

Beat 1 **egg yolk** with 1 tablespoon **milk**. With a very soft brush, paint tops of brioches; do not let egg accumulate in joint of topknot.

Bake in 425° oven for about 20 minutes or until richly browned.

Remove from pans and serve warm, or cool on wire racks and serve at room temperature. Package airtight to store (1 or 2 days at room temperature, several months in freezer). To reheat rolls (thawed, if frozen), set on a baking sheet and place in a 350° oven for 10 minutes. Makes 24.

Brioche with a head

(Brioche à tête)

A large-scale version of the individual brioche, this bread is an impressive offering. You can serve slices of it with butter and jam for breakfast, or serve it as a dinner bread.

Prepare 1 recipe's worth **brioche dough** (preceding); pinch off ⅙ and set aside. Shape large portion into a smooth ball by drawing surfaces of dough to underside.

Place in a well-buttered fluted brioche pan (page 7) that is about 9 inches across top or a 2-quart round baking pan. Pat dough down evenly into pan.

Shape small piece of dough into a teardrop shape, making top smooth as for larger piece. With your fingers, poke a hole in center of large dough portion through to pan bottom. Nest pointed end of small piece into hole; settle in securely or topknot will topple during baking.

Cover with a clear plastic film and let stand in a warm place until about double in bulk (takes 1 to 2 hours). Remove cover.

Beat 1 **egg yolk** with 1 tablespoon **milk**; brush over surface of brioche, taking care to prevent egg from accumulating in crack of topknot.

Bake in a 350° oven for about 1 hour or until a wooden skewer inserted in center comes out clean. Let stand 5 minutes; then invert carefully from pan. Serve warm, or cool on wire rack. (Freeze to store.) To reheat, set on flat pan (thawed, if frozen) in 325° oven for 30 minutes. Makes 1 loaf.

Croissants

(Croissants)

In France, bakers begin the creation of these crescent-shaped, flaky, nonsweet, yeast-perfumed rolls in the wee hours of the day, so they can grace breakfast tables—alone or in the company of petite brioches (page 85).

We recommend making croissants the day before and reheating for any meal—breakfast, lunch, or dinner.

Bring 1 cup (½ lb.) **butter** or margarine to room temperature while you prepare yeast dough.

Soften 1 package **active dry yeast** in ¼ cup **warm water** (about 110°); blend with ¾ cup warm **milk**, 1 tablespoon **sugar**, ½ teaspoon **salt**, and 2¾ cups unsifted **all-purpose flour**. Stir until flour is moistened and dough holds together.

Turn dough out on board coated with **all-purpose flour** and knead until smooth and velvety (takes about 5 minutes).

Wash, dry, and grease mixing bowl; add dough and turn over to grease top. Cover with clear plastic film and let rise in a warm place until double in bulk (takes about 2 hours).

(If you have a dough hook, simply mix ingredients until dough pulls cleanly from sides of bowl —omit kneading and don't grease bowl.)

Punch dough down and knead to expel air bubbles (or stir with dough hook).

Roll on a floured board to form a rectangle about ¼ inch thick. Cut butter in slices (it should be just soft enough to spread on a firm bread, but not meltingly soft) and arrange slices in center ⅓ section of dough rectangle. Fold each extending side over butter, pressing and sealing edges together where they meet.

Roll out again on floured board until rectangle is about ⅜ inch thick; turn dough over occasionally, flouring board lightly to prevent sticking. Fold in thirds again to make a squarish rectangle. Roll dough and fold again in exactly the same manner. At all times, take care not to pierce or tear dough surface.

(If at any time dough oozes butter and becomes sticky while you're rolling it, dust area with flour, then chill dough until butter is firmer.)

Wrap dough in clear plastic film and chill for 15 to 30 minutes. Roll and fold as directed before. Chill dough wrapped, for 15 to 20 minutes. Then roll and fold again and chill as directed.

Roll dough into a rectangle that is 7 inches wide and 36 inches long (dough is springy, so roll it out a bit more to end up with these dimensions).

BREADS YOU CAN MAKE at home are the province of the baker in France: long, crisp baguettes; top-knotted small and large brioches; flaky, crescent-shaped croissants.

On one long side, mark 6-inch intervals on dough. On other long side, make a mark at 3 inches, then at 6-inch intervals thereafter. With a long, sharp, flour-dusted knife, make a cut straight down from first 3-inch mark to 6-inch mark opposite.

Then, keeping knife tip at 3-inch mark, make a second cut at next 6-inch mark. This makes a triangle. Repeat cuts, following this pattern, to make 11 large triangles and 2 smaller triangles. Overlap straight-sided edges of small triangles and press lightly to join.

Starting at a 6-inch side, pull dough out to make it about 8 inches, then roll up from this side without stretching dough. Pinch tip to body of roll to secure. Set roll, tip side under, on an ungreased baking sheet; pull ends in to form a U or crescent shape.

Repeat to make each croissant, spacing about 2 inches apart.

Cover lightly and let rise in a warm, draft-free place. When about doubled in bulk (takes 1 to 2 hours), uncover and brush each roll gently with mixture of 1 **egg yolk** beaten with 1 tablespoon **milk**.

Bake in a 375° oven for 25 minutes or until golden brown. (Croissants served in Paris are usually a deeper brown than we bake rolls. If you want to duplicate French style, bake croissants 5 to 7 minutes more.) Serve hot, or cool on wire racks and package airtight. Refrigerate for as long as 2 days, or freeze (thaw to reheat). Reheat on a flat pan in a 350° oven for 8 minutes. Makes 12 croissants.

Savarin

(Savarin)

A liqueur-flavored syrup soaks into the springy, faintly sweet yeast dessert that is a cross between a bread and a cake. The thin yeast batter is stirred together, allowed to rise, stirred again to expel air, and poured into a decorative mold for baking.

Mix 1 package **active dry yeast** with ¼ cup **warm water** (about 110°) and let stand about 5 minutes to soften.

With an electric mixer beat ½ cup (¼ lb.) room-temperature **butter** or margarine with 3 tablespoons **sugar** and ½ teaspoon **salt**. Add 4 **eggs**, one at a time, blending well. Add ½ cup **warm milk**, yeast mixture, and 2 cups unsifted **all-purpose flour** and beat until well blended (or mix vigorously with a heavy spoon).

Cover with clear plastic film and let rise about 1½ hours in a warm place until doubled in volume. Stir vigorously to remove air bubbles.

Butter heavily a 10-cup tube pan with permanent bottom (such as a savarin ring or bundt pan).

(Continued on next page)

Scatter ½ cup **sliced almonds** in pan, tilting pan so nuts cling all over buttered surface.

Pour in yeast batter. Cover again and let rise in a warm place about 1 hour or until again almost double in size.

Bake, uncovered, in a 400° oven for 30 minutes or until savarin begins to pull from pan sides. Let cool about 10 minutes; invert onto a wire rack, leaving pan over cake, and then tip cake back into pan (this frees cake so it will be easy to remove later).

Pierce surface of savarin about every ½ inch with a fork. Pour **savarin syrup** (directions follow) onto cake. Let stand until warm or at room temperature (until next day, if desired; freeze for longer storage).

Invert savarin onto a serving plate. Cut in wedges and serve plain, with slightly **sweetened whipped cream** (and berries or sliced fruit such as peaches), or with Chantilly custard (page 80). Makes about 10 servings.

Savarin syrup. Combine 2½ cups **sugar**, 2 cups **water**, 1 teaspoon grated **orange peel**, and ½ teaspoon slightly crushed **coriander seed** (optional). Bring to a boil, stirring, until clear and sugar is dissolved. Remove from heat and add ¼ cup (or to taste) **rum**, cointreau, Grand Marnier, or kirsch. Use hot or cold, pouring onto savarin through a wire strainer to remove seeds and peel.

Chocolate mayonnaise
(Mayonnaise au chocolat)

It would seem that French cooks vie with one another to see who can create the richest, smoothest, chocolatiest mousse. A forerunner in any competition is this version. An economical tip is included for turning regular butter into sweet butter, a technique to make use of frequently if you prefer eating and cooking with sweet butter.

Beat at high speed with an electric mixer 1 cup (½ lb.) room-temperature **sweet butter** or washed butter (directions follow) with ¾ cup **sugar** until light and fluffy in texture.

Melt 1½ cups (8 oz.) **semisweet chocolate**, then add to butter and continue to beat at high speed until blended. Still at high speed, beat in 6 **eggs**, one at a time, until thoroughly blended. Spoon into a serving bowl or individual dishes and chill, covered, as long as 3 days (freeze for longer storage). Makes 8 to 10 servings.

Washed butter. To remove salt from regular butter so that it may be used in place of more costly and highly perishable sweet butter, follow this procedure: Cut **butter** in chunks and cover with **cold tap water**. Slowly mix with an electric mixer, or mash butter with a wooden spoon, working water into butter.

Drain off water and repeat washing 3 or 4 times or until butter no longer tastes salty. Mix, or work, drained butter to force out pockets of water, draining as it accumulates. Cover and chill until ready to use for cooking or serving with bread.

Mocha cake
(Gâteau moka)

A mildly sweetened, lightly flavored, rather hard cooky called "petit beurre" (available in well-stocked supermarkets) is the base of this no-cook cake. Or you can use tea biscuits or shortbread cookies.

With an electric mixer beat 1 cup (½ lb.) room-temperature **butter** or margarine, 1 teaspoon grated **orange peel**, and 3 cups sifted **powdered sugar** until fluffy. Then beat in 2 **egg yolks**, one at a time, whipping until mixture is very smooth and light. Blend ¼ cup **ground sweet chocolate** and 1 teaspoon **instant coffee powder** with 2 teaspoons **hot water**, then add to butter mixture and mix thoroughly; set aside.

Divide 1 package (7 to 9 oz.—24 to 30 cookies) **petit beurre**, tea biscuits, or shortbread cookies into 3 equal stacks. Arrange cookies from first stack side by side on a flat serving dish to form a rectangle or square. Sprinkle with 1 tablespoon hot or cold **coffee** and spread with a little less than ⅓ of butter cream mixture.

Arrange cookies from second stack on butter cream, sprinkle with another 1 tablespoon **coffee**, and spread with a little less than ⅓ of butter cream. Place cookies from third stack over this layer of butter cream and moisten evenly with 1 more tablespoon **coffee**. Frost top and sides of rectangle with remaining butter cream (or reserve a small amount for decoration).

Lightly dust 1 or 2 tablespoons **ground sweet chocolate** over top of cake; decorate, if you wish, with puffs of reserved butter cream. Chill at least 3 hours or as long as 3 days before serving; cover after butter cream gets firm. (Freeze for longer storage; thaw in refrigerator.) Cut in squares or rectangles to serve. Makes 8 to 12 servings.

Lemon ice
(Glace au citron)

Freeze ice in reamed lemon shells for an attractive presentation. The ice can be a dessert or a refreshing pause between a fish course and a meat dish— should you elect to dine more formally.

The ice is also a superb topping for wedges of honeydew melon.

Grate 2 tablespoons **lemon peel**, taking care not to get any white part. Combine peel with 1½ cups **sugar** and 2 cups **water**. Cover and let stand at least 4 hours.

Stir to mix sugar into liquid and pour through a wire strainer; discard peel. Add to syrup ½ cup unstrained (seeded) **orange juice** and ¾ cup unstrained (seeded) **lemon juice**.

Pour liquid into a shallow metal pan (for fast freezing). Freeze at 0° or colder until firm.

Remove from freezer and let stand until you can break ice into chunks. Then beat slowly with an electric mixer, working up to high speed as ice turns into a creamy slush. Pour back into pan (or container with cover, or lemon shells) and return to freezer until hard. Serve; or wrap airtight and store as long as 2 months. Makes about 2½ cups; ⅓ to ½ cup makes a portion.

Orange ice
(Glace à l'orange)

Citrus peel steeped in the syrup gives these ices their remarkably fresh, natural flavor.

Follow directions for **lemon ice** (preceding) but use **orange peel** instead of lemon peel; reduce **sugar** to 1¼ cups and **water** to 1 cup. Use 1½ cups **orange juice** and only 2 tablespoons **lemon juice**. Makes about 3 cups; allow ½ cup for a serving.

Strawberry or raspberry sorbet
(Sorbet aux fraises ou aux framboises)

A sorbet is often served with fresh fruit; berries, stone fruits, grapes, pineapple, and oranges are a few choices.

For further variation in this recipe, use a combination of strawberries and raspberries.

In a blender or food processor, whirl smooth, a portion at a time, 4 cups **strawberries** or raspberries (or force through a food mill); pour through a wire strainer to remove seeds. Add ½ cup **orange juice** and **sugar** to taste (about ⅓ cup). Pour into a shallow metal pan and freeze at 0° or colder until solid.

Remove from freezer and let sorbet stand at room temperature until you can break it up with a spoon. Beat with an electric mixer, slowly at first; then when pieces are small, beat at high speed to a smooth slush. Pour into container, package airtight, and return to freezer; store as long as 2 months. Serve in scoops, when desired. Makes about 1 quart; allow ½ cup for a serving.

Macaroons
(Macarons)

This chewy, golden cooky is easy to make with almond paste. Unlike most recipes, this one calls for egg white to be measured to assure proper consistency for the dough.

With an electric mixer, blend ½ pound (about 1 cup) **almond paste** with 1 cup **sugar**. Add ¼ cup **egg white** (about 2 egg whites) and beat until mixture is smooth. Batter should be stiff enough to hold its shape without flowing. (Add a little more egg white, 1 teaspoon at a time, if mixture is too stiff to put through a force bag; add a little more sugar if mixture is too soft.)

Squeeze through a force bag with large plain round tip onto greased and flour-dusted baking sheet. Make each macaroon about 1-tablespoon size, and leave 1 inch between cookies. (Or you can shape 1-tablespoon balls of batter, place on baking sheet, and flatten slightly.)

Place a **blanched whole almond** on top of each cooky.

Bake in a 350° oven for 20 to 25 minutes or until golden. Let cool 5 minutes, then free from pan with a spatula and place on wire racks to cool. Store airtight up to a week at room temperature; freeze for longer storage. Makes about 3 dozen.

Madeleines
(Madeleines)

You hear a number of stories about the origin of madeleines. The most plausible has to do with a French pastry chef who decided to bake pound cake batter in pretty aspic molds. The results were so well received that now pans are made expressly for madeleines, with scallop-shaped wells that give the form (page 7). Serve these little cakes as you would a cooky.

With an electric mixer, beat 1 cup (½ lb.) room-temperature **butter** or margarine until fluffy, gradually adding 2½ cups sifted **powdered sugar**. Add 4 **eggs**, one at a time, beating at high speed after each addition. Add 2 cups unsifted **all-purpose flour** and ¼ teaspoon **lemon extract** and mix thoroughly.

Generously **butter** and **flour**-dust cups in a madeleine pan. Fill each cup with 1½ tablespoons batter.

Bake in a 350° oven for 20 to 25 minutes or until cakes are lightly browned. Remove from oven and immediately turn madeleines out of pan to cool. (If you have only one pan, wash, dry, butter, and flour-dust to use again; meanwhile, batter can stand at room temperature.)

Store madeleines airtight at room temperature up to 1 week; freeze for longer storage. Makes 3 dozen.

Pine nut crescents
(Croissants aux pignons)

This cooky is typical of pâtisseries in Provence. The crescents are brushed with honey as a subtle complement to the faintly resinous flavor of the nuts. Orange flower water is found in liquor stores.

Beat together 1 cup (½ lb.) room-temperature **butter** or margarine and ⅔ cup packed **light brown sugar**. Add 3 **egg yolks**, one at a time, blending well. Stir in 1 teaspoon *each* grated **orange peel** and **orange flower water** (optional), ½ teaspoon **vanilla**, and 2¾ cups unsifted **all-purpose flour**.

To make each cooky, measure a 1-tablespoon portion of dough. Roll dough between lightly floured palms into a rope about 2½ inches long. Shape into a crescent on a well-greased baking sheet. Repeat to make each crescent. Leave about a 2-inch space between cookies.

Press **pine nuts** (½ cup total) onto surfaces of cookies.

In a small pan, warm 3 tablespoons **honey**, stirring. Brush honey gently onto cookies; press back in place any dislodged pine nuts. Take care to get as little honey on pan as possible, as it will scorch.

Bake in a 325° oven for 15 minutes or until golden. At once, slip a spatula under cookies, working gently to free. Cool cookies on wire racks. Store airtight as long as a week; freeze for longer storage. Makes about 3½ dozen.

Gaufrettes
(Gaufrettes)

Thin, crisp cookies are baked over direct heat in a cooky iron that goes by the same name (page 7); you can use a krumkake or pizzelle iron as a substitute.

Leave cookies flat, or while still warm and pliable, roll into cylinders.

Beat 1 cup **whipping cream** just until it begins to thicken; then blend in 1 cup unsifted **all-purpose flour**, ¾ cup unsifted **powdered sugar**, 2 teaspoons **vanilla**, and ¼ teaspoon **salt**.

Place a gaufrette iron (or other cooky iron) directly over medium-high heat. Alternately heat both sides of iron until water dripped inside sizzles.

Open iron and brush lightly with melted **butter** or margarine.

Spoon about 2 tablespoons batter (less for krumkake or pizzelle irons, which are smaller) down center of buttered iron; close and squeeze handles together. Turn iron and scrape off any batter that flows out. Bake, turning about every 20 seconds, until cooky is light golden brown (takes 1½ to 2 minutes); open often to check doneness.

Working very quickly, lift out cooky with a fork or spatula; cut cooky in half crosswise and leave flat or roll at once to form a cylinder. (If first cooky sticks, use salt and a paper towel—no water —to scour iron clean; then continue.)

Leave iron on heat; repeat procedure to bake each cooky. Store airtight as long as 1 week; freeze for longer storage. Makes about 2 dozen.

Marzipan bonbons
(Massepains)

These uncooked confections are based on almond paste; you can use the marzipan mixture plain or combine with colored sugars, nuts, or dried fruits.

Beat ½ pound (about 1 cup) **almond paste** with ½ cup (¼ lb.) room-temperature **butter** or margarine until smoothly mixed. Stir in 3 cups unsifted **powdered sugar** and blend well.

Flavor or color and shape as desired, according to suggestions that follow.

(Marzipan can be covered and chilled until ready to use, as long as a month.)

To flavor, add to each ½ cup marzipan ¼ teaspoon **vanilla** or ½ teaspoon liqueur such as cointreau, rum, kahlúa, brandy, cognac, kirsch; work in well.

To color, add **food coloring** a drop or two at a time; work color in smoothly.

To shape, roll about 1-teaspoon-size portions of marzipan lightly between your palms, forming balls, logs, or ovals.

Serve plain or decorate. Roll in **finely chopped nuts**, whole pine nuts, colored sugars, or chocolate shot, pressing lightly to make coatings stick.

Or nest marzipan in hollows of **pitted prunes**, or sandwich between dried apricots or pecan or walnut halves.

Wrap finished confections airtight; do not stack. Refrigerate up to 1 month (from initial mixing of marzipan) or freeze for longer storage. Serve chilled or at room temperature.

Makes about 2⅓ cups or enough for about 100 confections, each made with 1 teaspoon marzipan.

Chestnut mousse
(Mousse aux marrons)

The mellow, smooth flavor of this creamy mousse is complemented by fresh or frozen raspberries.

(Continued on page 92)

AFTERNOON TEA with sweets is a custom with the French (though perhaps less constant than for the English); from upper right down: madeleines, pine nut crescents, macaroons, marzipan bonbons, and gaufrettes.

With an electric mixer at high speed, beat 5 **egg yolks** until very thick and light in color. At same time, boil in a small pan over highest heat ⅔ cup **sugar** and ⅓ cup **water** until 234° or at spin-a-thread stage.

Pour hot syrup slowly into yolks (not into beaters, as they spin syrup onto bowl sides), mixing at high speed. Then beat in ½ cup (¼ lb.) room-temperature **butter** or margarine, 1 teaspoon **vanilla**, and 2 tablespoons **cointreau** (or other orange-flavored liqueur).

Wash and dry beaters and beat 5 **egg whites** at high speed until stiff, then gradually beat in ¾ cup **sugar** until whites hold high, distinct peaks when beaters are lifted. With same beaters (unwashed) whip ½ cup **whipping cream** until stiff.

Fold whites, yolks, cream with 1 can (15½ oz.) unsweetened chestnut purée, blending well. Pour into an 8 or 9-inch straight-sided dish at least 2 inches deep (or pan with removable bottom that does not leak).

Cover and freeze at 0° or colder until firm (at least 8 hours or as long as 2 months).

Let mousse stand in refrigerator 15 to 20 minutes before serving. (If desired, you can remove pan rim by wrapping it in a hot, wet cloth just long enough to slightly melt side; run a knife blade around inside edge and remove rim.)

Scoop out portions of mousse (or cut in wedges if pan rim is removed).

Top servings with **sugared raspberries** (you'll need about 2 cups). Makes 12 to 16 servings.

Chestnut cream with berries

(*Crème aux marrons avec baies*)

Fresh cream and berries turn a convenient canned product into a noteworthy dessert.

Open 1 can (about 8 oz.) **chestnut spread** and spoon equally into 4 small dessert dishes.

Pour 2 or 3 tablespoons **whipping cream** (½ to ¾ cup total) into each dish, then top with a few fresh or frozen **raspberries**, strawberries, or blueberries (about 1 to 1½ cups fruit). Makes 4 servings.

Gâteau St. Honoré

(*Gâteau Saint-Honoré*)

The patron saint of bakers, St. Honoratus of Amiens, is honored by this cake named for him. There are many versions, but all combine cream puffs and pastry assembled in a cakelike shape with a creamy filling in the center.

If you want, make just cream puffs and fill them with sweetened whipped cream for a separate dessert.

Measure 1 cup **short paste** (page 93) and press evenly over bottom of a 9 or 10-inch cheesecake pan with removable sides.

Bake in a 325° oven for 30 minutes or until light golden brown; cool.

Select enough **cream puffs** (directions follow) to make a close-fitting ring against pan rim on crust; set aside.

Mix 1 envelope **unflavored gelatin** in ¼ cup **cold water** and let stand about 5 minutes to soften. Set over **hot water** and stir to dissolve completely.

Separate 4 **eggs** and put whites in a large mixing bowl, yolks in a smaller bowl.

With an electric mixer at high speed, beat whites until foamy, then gradually add ¼ cup **sugar**, beating until whites hold soft shiny peaks when beater is lifted; set aside.

Without washing beater, beat egg yolks with an additional ¼ cup **sugar** until they are thick. Mix in dissolved gelatin, ¼ cup **rum**, and 1 teaspoon **vanilla**.

Also beat 1 cup **whipping cream** until soft peaks form.

Fold together whipped whites, egg yolk mixture, and whipped cream.

In a small bowl, smoothly blend 1½ tablespoons *each* **cocoa** and **water**. Spoon 1½ cups of the rum cream mixture into cocoa and fold to blend evenly.

Pinching to open slashed side, fill each cream puff with plain rum cream. Spoon remaining plain rum cream onto pastry crust and spread evenly. Set filled cream puffs on top, with cut sides facing center. Spoon chocolate mixture into center.

Cover and chill until firm (about 3 hours), or until next day. Run a knife around edge and remove rim of pan. If desired, garnish with curls of **semi-sweet chocolate**. Cut in wedges. Makes about 10 or 12 servings.

Cream puffs. In a small pan combine ½ cup **water**, 4 tablespoons **butter** or margarine, and 1 teaspoon **sugar**. Bring to a boil and, when butter melts, add all at once ½ cup unsifted **all-purpose flour**.

Remove from heat and mix until dough holds together (or mix in food processor). Add 2 **eggs**, one at a time, beating vigorously after each addition until smooth and glossy. Let cool about 15 minutes. (This is the classic **pâte à choux**.)

For each puff, spoon 1 tablespoon dough at a time onto a lightly greased baking sheet; keep about 1 inch apart.

Bake in a 375° oven for about 30 minutes or until firm and dry to touch and well browned. Slash sides of each puff about halfway through while hot; place puffs on wire rack to cool. (Wrap airtight and freeze if you want to store for longer than 12 hours.) Makes 12 to 14.

Paris crown

(Paris-Brest)

In pâtisseries you see this dessert made as a large cake to cut and serve, or in tiny individual rings. It is a Parisian specialty.

Prepare paste for **cream puff** (page 92) and place in a pastry bag with a large rosette or plain tip. Force paste through tip onto a greased baking sheet, making a ring that is about 1½ inches thick and 8 inches in outside diameter.

Bake in a 375° oven for about 50 minutes or until rich golden brown. Slide onto a wire rack and while hot, slice off horizontally the top ⅓, pushing slightly aside so ring will stay crisp as it cools. (Wrap airtight and freeze if you want to hold for more than 12 hours.)

Beat 1 cup **whipping cream** until soft peaks form, add **sugar** to taste, and flavor with ½ teaspoon **vanilla** or liqueur to taste (or use uncooked pastry cream, page 94, or cooked pastry cream, page 94).

If you like, spoon about ½ to 1 cup lemon butter (page 94) in base of cooled pastry ring. Fill with cream (you can force whipped cream through a pastry bag with large rosette tip for a more decorative effect). Set top of pastry in place. Pastry is most crisp when just assembled, but can be covered and chilled until next day.

Dust with **powdered sugar** and cut in wide slices. Makes 6 to 8 servings.

Fresh fruit tarts

(Tartes aux fruits frais)

Raw fruit or cooked fruit carefully arranged about one layer deep on the surface of tarts—one-bite-size to party-size desserts—are attractive, seasonal, and quick to make if you keep pastry shells of short paste (directions follow) on hand in the freezer. Make a layer of a creamy filling in the bottom of the shell before adding the fruit (three choices follow); the filling helps hold the fruit in place when serving—and tastes good, too.

Suitable fruits include strawberries, raspberries, blueberries, loganberries, currants, or other bush berries; sliced plums, peaches, nectarines, apricots, or pitted cherries (fruits that darken should be dipped in lemon juice before being placed on tart); sliced figs; cooked apple or pear slices; thinly sliced oranges or pineapple; seedless or seeded grapes. Use any colorful combination. You can leave the fruit plain, sprinkle it with granulated (plain or vanilla) **sugar** or powdered sugar, or brush it with melted jelly for a shiny finish.

Serve within 2 or 3 hours of final assembly; keep cold during interim.

How much fruit to use. A berry or two or a slice of fruit is adequate for a 2-inch tart; 3 to 5-inch tarts need ½ to 1 cup fruit; 6 or 7-inch tarts, 2 cups fruit; 8 or 9-inch tarts, 3 cups fruit; 10 or 11-inch tarts, 4 cups fruit; and 12-inch tarts, at least 6 cups fruit.

How much filling to use. A spoonful in small tarts is adequate; fill 3 to 5-inch tarts about half full; larger tarts can accommodate 1 to 2 cups filling.

Short paste

(Pâte brisée)

This pastry benefits from lots of handling, unlike pie dough.

Stir together 2 cups unsifted **all-purpose flour** and ¼ cup **sugar**. Add ¾ cup (⅜ lb.) **butter** or margarine, cut in chunks. Crumble mixture with your fingers until of even texture. With a fork, stir in 2 **egg yolks** (for more golden dough) or 1 whole egg. Stir until dough holds together. With your hands, press dough firmly to make a smooth shiny ball; warmth of your hands helps to blend dough.

To shape, press measured amount of pastry into pan or pans, pushing it firmly to make an even layer, with edge flush with pan rim. Allow about 1 teaspoon dough for tiny one-bite-size tarts in pans 2 inches wide and about ¼ inch deep; 2 to 3 tablespoons dough for individual tarts in pans 3 to 5 inches wide and about 1 inch deep; ¼ to ½ cup dough for tart pans 6 to 7 inches wide and about 1 inch deep; about 1 cup dough for an 8 to 9-inch tart pan (or pie pan); about 1½ cups dough for an 11-inch tart pan; and 2 cups dough for a 12-inch pan.

Bake pastry in a 300° oven for 20 to 30 minutes (depending on size) until lightly browned.

Let pastries cool in pan. Invert small tarts and tap lightly to free; set cup side up.

For larger tarts that you want to serve outside of pan, use pans with removable sides.

(Continued on next page)

"Behind such an open face, one finds a sweet secret!"

Dough can be covered and refrigerated as long as 1 week. Cooked pastries, wrapped airtight, can be kept at room temperature 3 to 4 days; freeze for longer storage. Makes 2 cups dough.

Cooked pastry cream
(Crème frangipane)

This filling can also be used for cream puffs and éclairs.

In a small pan mix ⅓ cup **sugar** with 1 tablespoon **cornstarch** and ⅔ cup **milk**. Bring to a boil, stirring, until thickened and smooth. Remove sauce from heat and at once stir in 1 **egg yolk** (save white for other uses). Flavor sauce with 1½ tablespoons **kirsch** or 1 teaspoon vanilla. Cover pan and chill sauce as long as 2 days, if you like.

Beat ⅓ cup **whipping cream** until stiff and fold into cooled sauce. Makes about 1½ cups.

Uncooked pastry cream
(Crème pâtissière)

As no cooking is required, this sauce is useful when you are in a hurry.

Place 1 small package (3 oz.) **cream cheese** in a bowl and beat at high speed with an electric mixer; gradually blend in 1 cup **whipping cream**. Add ½ teaspoon *each* **vanilla** and grated **lemon peel** and 1 teaspoon **lemon juice**. Beat until mixture is like stiffly whipped cream. Add **sugar** to taste.

Chill, covered, until ready to use (within 24 hours). Or you can spoon filling into **pastry shells** and chill, covered, as long as 24 hours.

Lemon butter
(Beurre au citron)

Lemon butter is good alone as a filling for small tarts; it can also be topped with fruit in small or large tarts. You can use lemon butter as a sauce, too, for uniced cake slices, ice cream, or poached plums. Try it as filling for a layer cake.

In top of a double boiler melt ½ cup (¼ lb.) **butter** or margarine. Add 1 teaspoon grated **lemon peel**, ½ cup **lemon juice**, 1¼ cups **sugar**, and 4 **eggs**, beating to blend thoroughly.

Cook about 20 minutes over **simmering water**, stirring, until thickened and smooth. Pour through a fine wire strainer if you want to remove peel.

Chill, covered. Keeps 2 weeks in refrigerator. Makes 2 cups.

FINAL COMPLEMENT for quickly made hot apple pastry is dollop of cool, thick, tangy crème fraîche. Additional accessories are jelly and applesauce.

Hot apple or pear tarts
(Tartes chaudes aux pommes ou aux poires)

Frozen puff patty shells, thawed and rolled thin, are the base of these remarkably quick and delicious individual fruit tarts.

To make each serving, roll 1 thawed, frozen **puff patty shell** out on a floured board to make 5 to 6-inch circle. Place on an ungreased baking sheet.

Peel, core, and thinly slice half of a medium-size **apple** or pear and arrange fruit slices over pastry. Sprinkle with 1 or 2 teaspoons **sugar**.

Bake in a 400° oven for 20 to 25 minutes or until crust is a rich golden brown. Two or 3 minutes before removing pastry from oven, put about 2 teaspoons **jelly** (currant, apple, or other berry) on center of tart. At end of baking time, remove from oven and brush melted jelly over surface of pastry.

Serve hot with spoonfuls of **crème fraîche** (page 77) or whipped cream, **applesauce** (optional), and **jelly** (optional) alongside. Eat with knife and fork. Makes 1 serving.

Index

Alsatian stew, 48
Anchoiade provençale, 14
Apéritifs: a refreshing way to begin, 9
Artichauts florentins, 64
Artichauts vinaigrettes, 11
Artichokes florentine, 64
Artichokes vinaigrette, 11
Asparagus, 58
Asparagus, hot or cold with sauces, 64
Asperges, 64
Assorted vegetable salads, 9
Assortiment de crudités, 9

Baguettes, 84
Basic crêpes, 81
Basic steak sauté, 58
Bean casserole with salted duck, 43
Beans, 65
Béarnaise, 70
Béchamel sauce, 70
Beckenoffe, 48
Beef
  in casserole, 55
  fillet, 55, 58, 62
  patties, 59
  steak, 58, 61, 62
  stew, 52
  tongue, 50
  with vegetables, 52
Beef fillet with vegetable bouquet for two, 58
Beef in casserole, 55
Beet salad, 9
Berries, with chestnut cream, 92
Beurre au citron, 94
Blanquette de veau ou ragoût à l'ancienne, 48
Boeuf bourguignon, 52
Boeuf en croûte, 55
Boeuf en daube, 55
Boiled beef with vegetables, 52
Boiled flageolets, 65
Boiled tongue, 49
Boiled white beans, 65
Bonbons, marzipan, 90
Bouillabaisse, 30
Bourbonnaise dressing, 71
Braised leeks, 66
Bread, French, 19
Breads, 83–87
Brioche à tête, 85
Brioche dough, 84
Brioche, salmon in, 27
Brioches, individual, 85
Brioche with a head, 85
Brittany-style onion-stuffed chicken, 33
Broth, clarified, 49
Bulgur wheat filling, 28
Burgundy-style beef stew, 52
Butter bercy, 58
Butter cream crêpes with jam, 81
Butters
  bercy, 58
  lemon, 94
  parsley, 51
  washed, 88

Cabbage, red, with pork, 45
Cake, mocha, 88
Cailles à la sauce vignoble, 42
Canard à l'orange, 42
Canard au poivre vert, 40
Canard aux olives, 39
Caramel custard, 80
Carottes à la vichy, 64
Carottes rapées, 9
Carré d'agneau à la sauce au genièvre, 51
Carrot salad, shredded, 9
Carrots, sugar-glazed, 58
Carrots vichy, 64
Casseroles, 43, 55
Cassoulet au confit de canard, 43

Cassoulet without confit, 43
Cauliflower mornay, 64
Cauliflower soup, 19
Caviar, 13
Céleri remoulade, 9
Celery root salad, 9
Champignons à la crème, 66
Chantilly custard, 80
Chateaubriand à la bouquetière pour deux, 58
Cheese and eggs, 71–82
Cheese crusted chicken with cream (see cover photo), 33
Cheese quiches or cheese tarts, 77
Cheese ramekins, 73
Cheese salad Androuët, 73
Cheese, the, 71
Chestnut cream with berries, 92
Chestnut mousse, 90
Chestnut soufflé, 64
Chicken, 33–35, 38–40
Chicken breasts veronique, 34
Chicken breast with shrimp sauce, 34
Chicken cordon bleu, 35
Chicken kiev, 35
Chicken liver pâté, 11
Chicken marengo, 38
Chicken sauté with shallots, 38
Chicken with Beaujolais, 40
Chicken with green olives, 39
Chicken with port cream, 39
Chicken with Riesling, 35
Chicken with tarragon cream, 39
Chocolate mayonnaise, 88
Choucroute garnie, 45
Chou-fleur mornay, 45
Citrus crêpes, 82
Clams bordelaise, 29
Clarifying broth, 16
Coeurs à la crème, 76
Cold, cooked shellfish, 14
Cold meats, 13
Confit de canard, 43
Confit: salt-preserved duck, 43
Consommé, 16
Cooked pastry cream, 94
Cooked sauces, 70
Cookies, 89–90
Coq au Beaujolais, 40
Coq au Riesling, 35
Coq au vin, 40
Coq au vin blanc, 35
Coquilles Saint-Jacques à la provençale, 29
Coquilles Saint-Jacques au gratin, 28
Cornichons: little green pickles, 13
Côtelette kiev, 35
Country omelet, 76
Country terrine with aspic, 11
Crab omelet, 74
Creamed sorrel, 68
Creamed spinach, 68
Cream hearts, 76
Cream of mushroom soup, 17
Cream puffs, 92
Crème anglaise, 79
Crème anglaise à la Chantilly, 80
Crème aux marrons avec baies, 92
Crème de champignons, 17
Crème fraîche, 77
Crème fraîche dressing, 71
Crème fraîche, eggs with, 73
Crème frangipane, 94
Crème pâtisserie, 94
Crème renversée au caramel, 80
Crêpes, 81–82
Crêpes à la crème au beurre avec confiture, 81
Crêpes mylene, 81
Crêpes Suzette, 82
Crevettes à la bordelaise, 29
Croissants, 87
Croissants aux pignons, 90
Cucumber salad, 11
Custard, 80
Custard sauce, 79

Desserts, 87–94
Dordogne dressing, 71
Dressings, 9, 71

Drouant's veal kidneys on skewers, 50
Duckling, 39, 40, 42, 43
Duckling with green olives, 39
Duckling with orange sauce, 42
Dumplings, fish, 22
Duxelles, 57

Eggs and cheese, 71–82
Eggs with crème fraîche, 73
Eggs with hamburgers, 59
Eggs with snails on toast, 74
Eggs with watercress mayonnaise, 74
Emulsion sauces, 68–70
Épaule d'agneau farcie à la provençale, 51
Épinards à la crème, 68
Escargots à la bourguignonne, 14

Filbert mayonnaise, 49
Fillet of beef in a crust, 55
First courses, 8–14
Fish and shellfish, 21–31
Fish dumplings, 22
Fish stew, Honfleur, 30
Fish terrine, 13
Fish with sorrel, 24
Flageolets, 65
Floating islands, 79
Foie à la lyonnaise, 50
French hamburgers, 59
Fresh-fruit tarts, 93
Fromage à l'ail et aux fines herbes, 76
Fromage blanc, 77
Fruit, 93

Game and poultry, 32–43
Garlic and herb cheese, 76
Garnishing a terrine, 12
Gâteau moka, 88
Gâteau St. Honoré, 92
Gaufrettes, 90
Gigot à la Miche, 52
Gigot Port Saint-Germain, 51
Glace à l'orange, 89
Glace au citron, 88
Glace de viande, 16
Glazed parsnips, 66
Glazes, 16, 61
Grand Marnier soufflé, 82
Gratin, tomatoes, 70
Green beans gratin, 65
Green beans polonaise, 65
Green beans with sauces, 65
Greenery, the, 71
Green pea soup, 17
Green pepper salad, 9
Growing sorrel for the kitchen, 69

Hamburger à la niçoise, 59
Hamburger à l'estragon, 59
Hamburger niçoise, 59
Hamburgers, 59
Hamburgers avec oeufs à cheval, 59
Hamburgers with eggs on horseback, 59
Ham, parsleyed, Burgundy-style, 46
Haricots blancs, 65
Haricots verts, 65
Haricots verts à la polonaise, 65
Haricots verts gratinés, 65
Herb omelet, 74
Herring salads, 14
Hollandaise, 69–70
Homard flamberge, 29
Honfleur fish stew, 30
Hors d'oeuvres, 8–14
Hot apple or pear tarts, 94
Housewife's dressing, 71
How to bone chicken breasts, 34
How to serve a meal French-style, 5

Ices, 88–89
Individual brioches, 85

Jambon persillé à la bourguignonne, 46
Juniper berry basting sauce, 51

Kidneys, veal, 50
Kitchen tools, 6–7

La garniture d'une terrine, 12
Lamb
  leg, 51, 52
  rack, 51
  shoulder, 51
  stew, 48, 54
Langue de boeuf à la provençale, 50
Langue de boeuf à la sauce gribiche, 50
Langue de boeuf bouillie, 49
Lapin à la moutarde, 36
Lapin aux champignons et au vin blanc, 36
Leeks, braised, 66
Leek soup, 20
Leeks with tarragon, 65
Leg of lamb, Port Saint Germain-style, 51
Lemon butter, 94
Lemon ice, 88
Lemon omelet soufflé, 82
Les fromages, 71
Les salades, 71
Les vinaigrettes, 71
Lettuce with peas, 66
Liver lyonnaise, 50
Lobster flamberge, 29

Macarons, 89
Macaroons, 89
Madame Morier's roast pork, 45
Madame Morier's roast veal, 46
Madeleines, 89
Marinated beet salad, 9
Marzipan bonbons, 90
Massepains, 90
Matelote d'Honfleur, 30
Mayonnaise, 69
Mayonnaise au chocolat, 88
Mayonnaise, chocolate, 88
Mayonnaise, filbert, 49
Mayonnaise, watercress, 69
Meat glaze, 16, 61
Meats, 13, 44–62
Melon, 13
Miche's leg of lamb, 52
Mocha cake, 88
Mornay sauce, 70
Mousse aux marrons, 90
Mousse, chestnut, 90
Mousseline sauce, 70
Mushrooms, 17, 23, 36, 38, 58, 66
Mushrooms boiled with cream, 66
Mushroom soup, cream of, 17

Nantua sauce, 22
Naturals, 13
Navarin à la printanière, 54

Oeufs à la neige, 79
Oeufs aux escargots sur canapés, 14
Oeufs durs à la crème, 73
Oeufs durs à la mayonnaise au cresson, 74
Oeufs pochés des vignerons, 73
Oignons à la glace de viande, 66
Oignons braisés, 66
Omelets, 74, 76, 82
Omelette aux fines herbes, 74
Omelette brayaude, 76
Omelette de crabe, 74
Omelettes à la crème et aux tomates, 74
Omelette soufflée au citron, 82
Onglet sauté aux oignons, 62
Onions
  slow-cooked, 66
  sugar-glazed, 58
Onion soup, 17
Onions with meat glaze, 66
Orange ice, 89

Oseille à la crème, 68
Oysters on the half shell, 13

Palourdes à la bordelaise, 29
Panais glacés, 66
Paris-Brest, 93
Paris crown, 93
Parsley butter, 51
Parsley dressing, 9
Parsleyed ham,
    Burgundy-style, 46
Pastry cream, 94
Pastry dough, 77
Pastry, rich, 57
Pâte à brioche, 84
Pâte à choux, 92
Pâte brisée, 93
Pâté, chicken liver, 11
Pâté de foies de volailles, 11
Paupiettes de veau, 47
Pea soup, 17
Peas with lettuce, 66
Petite coffee custards, 80
Petite marmite, 20
Petites brioches, 85
Petite vanilla custards, 80
Petits pois aux laitues, 66
Pickles, cornichons, 13
Pigeonneaux farcis sur
    canapés, 36
Pilaf, 68
Pine nut crescents, 90
Piperade, 75
Pipèrade à la basquaise, 75
Pistou mixture, 20
Poached eggs in red wine
    sauce, 73
Poached salmon, 25, 27
Poireaux à l'estragon, 65
Poireaux braisés, 66
Poisson à l'oseille, 24
Pommes de terre gratinées, 66
Porc au choux rouges, 45
Pork
    potted, 12
    roast, 45
    stew, 48
Pork with red cabbage, 45
Potage au cresson, 19
Potage de légumes, 19
Potage Dubarry, 19
Potage Saint-Germain, 17
Potatoes gratin, 66
Potatoes, mashed, 28, 58
Pot au feu, 52
Pots de crème à la vanille, 80
Pots de crème au café, 80
Potted pork from Tours, 12
Poularde farcie aux oignons
    à la bretonne, 33
Poulet à la crème d'estragon, 39
Poulet au porto, 39
Poulet aux olives, 39
Poulet bonne femme, 38
Poulet cordon bleu, 35
Poulet gratiné au fromage, 33
Poulet marengo, 38
Poulet rôti farci à l'oseille, 33

Poultry and game, 32–43
Provençal anchovy sauce, 14
Provençal vegetable soup
    with basil, 20

Quail with vine sauce, 42
Quenelles, 22
Quiche Lorraine, 79
Quiches au fromage ou tartes
    de fromage, 77

Rabbit in mustard sauce, 36
Rabbit in wine with
    mushrooms, 36
Rack of lamb with juniper
    sauce, 51
Radish salad, 9
Ragoût à l'ancienne, 48
Ramekins au fromage, 73
Raspberry sorbet, 89
Ratatouille, 68
Rich meat broth, 16
Rillettes de Tours, 12
Ris de veau en aspic à la
    mayonnaise noisette, 49
Roast chicken with sorrel
    stuffing, 33
Roast duckling with green
    peppercorn sauce, 40
Roast duckling with orange
    sauce, 42
Roast pork with prunes, 45
Rognons de veau à la Drouant
    en brochette, 50
Rôti de porc aux pruneaux, 45
Rôti de porc Madame Morier, 45
Rôti de veau Madame Morier, 46
Rôti de veau Orloff, 46

Salade de betteraves, 9
Salade de concombres, 11
Salade de fromage
    Androuët, 73
Salade de poivrons, 9
Salade de radis, 9
Salads, 9, 11, 14, 71, 73
Salmon in brioche, 27
Salmon
    poached, 25, 27
    smoked, 13
Salted duck:
    Rocamadour-style, 43
Salted duck with bean
    casserole, 43
Sauces
    anchovy provençal, 14
    béarnaise, 70
    béchamel, 70
    crab, 74
    custard, 79
    green peppercorn, 61
    hollandaise, 69–70
    hot, 30
    juniper berry, 51
    madeira, 57
    marrow, 61
    mayonnaise, 69
    mornay, 70

Sauces (cont'd.)
    mousseline, 70
    mustard, 46
    nantua, 22
    soubise, 47
    tuna, 47
    watercress mayonnaise, 69
Sauce vinaigrette, 9
Sauerkraut with all the
    trimmings, 45
Saumon en brioche, 27
Saumon poché, 25
Savarin, 87
Savarin syrup, 88
Scallops in shells, 28
Scallops provençal, 29
Shellfish and fish, 14, 21–31
Short paste, 93
Shredded carrot salad, 9
Shrimp bordelaise, 29
Shrimp, cooked, 34
Slow-cooked onions, 66
Smoked salmon, 13
Snails with eggs on toast, 14
Snails with herb butter, 14
Snow eggs or floating
    islands, 79
Sole bonne femme, 22
Sole curry, 22
Sole gratinée aux
    champignons, 23
Sole gratin with mushrooms, 23
Sole le duc, 22
Sole veronique, 24
Sole with grapes, 24
Sole with shallots in cream, 22
Sorbet aux fraises ou aux
    framboises, 89
Sorbet, strawberry or
    raspberry, 89
Sorrel, 24, 33, 68
    how to grow, 69
Soufflé au Grand Marnier, 82
Soufflé aux marrons, 64
Soufflés, 64, 82
Soupe à l'oignon gratinée, 17
Soupe au pistou, 20
Soupe aux poireaux, 20
Soupe aux tomates, 19
Soups, 15–20
Spinach, creamed, 68
Springtime lamb stew, 54
Squab, roast stuffed on toast, 36
Steak à la glace de viande, 61
Steak à la moelle, 61
Steak à la sauce moutarde, 62
Steak au poivre, 61
Steak au poivre vert, 61
Steak, basic sauté, 58
Steak marchand de vin, 61
Steak sauté, 58
Steak sauté with onions, 62
Steak with black pepper, 61
Steak with green peppercorn
    sauce, 61
Steak with marrow sauce, 61
Steak with meat glaze, 61
Steak with mustard sauce, 62
Steak with wine glaze, 61
Stews, 30, 48, 52, 54, 68

Strawberry sorbet, 89
Stuffed lamb shoulder,
    provençal, 51
Stuffed roast squab on toast, 36
Stuffed veal rolls, 47
Suprêmes de volaille sauce
    nantua, 34
Suprêmes de volaille
    veronique, 34
Sweetbreads in aspic with
    filbert mayonnaise, 49

Tarragon burger, 59
Tartes aux fruits frais, 93
Tartes chaudes aux pommes ou
    aux poires, 94
Tarts, 77, 93, 94
Terrine bardée de lard, 12
Terrine de campagne
    en gelée, 11
Terrine de poisson, 13
Terrines, 11-12, 13
    garnishing, 12
Tomates gratinées, 68
Tomato cream omelets, 74
Tomatoes gratin, 68
Tomato soup, 19
Tongue, boiled, 49
Tongue, provençal, 50
Tongue with gribiche sauce, 50
Tools, 6–7
Tournedos Héloïse, 62
Tournedos Rossini, 62
Tripe, Caen-style, 50
Tripes à la mode de Caen, 50
Trout with almonds, 25
Trout with butter sauce, 24
Truite à la meunière, 24
Truite amandine, 25

Uncooked pastry cream, 94

Veal
    kidneys, 50
    roast, 46
    stew, 48
    stuffed rolls, 47
Veal roast Orloff, 46
Veal with tuna sauce, 47
Veau à la sauce au thon, 47
Vegetables, 9, 52, 54, 58, 63–68
Vegetable soup, 19
Vegetable soup, provençal, 20
Vegetable stew, 68
Vinaigrette à la crème, 71
Vinaigrette bonne femme, 71
Vinaigrette de Bourbon, 71
Vinaigrette de Dordogne, 71

Washed butter, 88
Watercress mayonnaise, 69
Watercress soup, 19
White cheese, 77
White cheese with crème
    fraîche, 77
White stew of veal, pork or
    lamb, 48
Wines, 5
Wrapped terrine, 12

A Handy Metric Conversion Table

To change	To	Multiply By
ounces (oz.)	grams (g)	28
pounds (lbs.)	kilograms (kg)	0.45
teaspoons	milliliters (ml)	5
tablespoons	milliliters (ml)	15
fluid ounces (oz.)	milliliters (ml)	30
cups	liters (l)	0.24
pints (pt.)	liters (l)	0.47
quarts (qt.)	liters (l)	0.95
gallons (gal.)	liters (l)	3.8
Fahrenheit temperature (°F)	Celsius temperature (°C)	5/9 after subtracting 32